HANDS-ON
SERVICE IDEAS
FOR YOUTH
GROUPS

BY
STEVE CASE
AND
FRED CORNFORTH

D0038510

Group
Loveland, Colorado

Credits
Cover Art Director: Liz Howe
Cover Illustrator: Steve Hunter

ISBN 1-55945-789-9

10 9 8 7 6 5 4 3 2 1   04 03 02 01 00 99 98 97 96 95
Printed in the United States of America.

DEDICATION

To Debbie Case and Kelly Cornforth—the ones who have demonstrated to us what service is all about. Thanks for your patience in teaching us!

ACKNOWLEDGMENTS

Our paths crossed during seminary. Both of us had been involved in various forms of ministry with a service emphasis. Later we found that we continued to cross paths because our service activities intersected, even though we lived in different parts of the country. One evening as we talked about what God was doing in our personal lives and in our ministries, we felt compelled to put some of our ideas on paper. This book is the result of that conversation and focuses on service ideas. No longer will we go to our files and thumb through the disorganized scraps of paper with one more idea that we find on three other sheets of paper, too. It's time to find it on the bookshelf.

This is certainly not the first service-idea book. Tony Campolo's *Ideas for Social Action* has become a classic for youth leaders. Recently Peter Benson and Eugene Roehlkepartain's *Beyond Leaf Raking* has given a helpful emphasis on spiritual formation through service activities with a term they coin, "service-learning."

We would like to give a special thanks to the hundreds of young people who have shaped our perspective and have participated and demonstrated involvement in service. We've learned a lot and hope to continue the process. Thank you, Barry Ulloth and Dorothy Roberson, for sharing your insights based on your experiences.

We want to mention our gratitude to Desiree Zweigle for the design and layout of the book and to Donna Pontynen for being the copy editor. Special thanks to Jeff Wood for permission to use his song "We Are His Hands."

Steve says, "Thank you to Debbie for inspiration to dream bigger than what others think is possible. And thanks to Katie for reminding Dad that playtime is more important than typing one more idea right now. And a BIG thank you to God for 'putting this love in my heart.' (By the way, Fred, don't forget to call me tomorrow night about our next deadline!)"

Fred would like to say, "Thank you to my good friend and wife, Kelly, for her support, creativity, and typing skills. And I thank God for my two children, Kadie and Charlie. And also a special thank you to Jesus for giving me a purpose in life—to serve others in his name. (By the way, Steve, don't forget to call me tomorrow night about our next deadline!)"

CONTENTS

SECTION 1: ABOUT SERVICE AND YOUTH GROUPS

STAGES OF SERVICE INVOLVEMENT

What happens when a youth leader plans a service project and only two youth show up? This fear haunts many youth leaders, and most youth ministry veterans will admit that this nightmare will happen eventually. An understanding of how individuals become active in service and what they may become active in can guide the leader into an appropriate progression of service activities. It can also spur development towards a service lifestyle. A youth group enthusiastic about serving others is the result of intentional planning that exposes them to community and world-wide needs through a diversity of methods. The following stages show the progression, with examples for each stage. An index at the back of the book classifies each of the 101 service ideas according to their stage of service involvement.

Stage 1

Create an awareness of local and world-wide needs in each person in your group. This requires a variety of programs and ideas. In this first stage you are *informing* a person rather than having them *do* some type of service project.

Some examples of stage 1 service awareness activities are:

a. Have a Guest Speaker -- such as a teen pregnancy center director, a homeless person, your local mayor, or an AIDS victim, address your group and identify needs where volunteers can respond. Be sure to leave time for questions.

b. TV or Video -- There are many movies, news specials and videos that have been produced to inform others about specific community or global needs. Check your local library, video store or service agency.

c. Newspapers and Magazines -- Today's publications are filled with articles about great service opportunities. Photocopy an article that appeals to you and distribute it for discussion at your next meeting.

d. Tour -- Contact some type of helping agency in your area such as a runaway shelter or food bank and set an appointment time for your group to tour the facility. Visit two or three places on a weekend afternoon.

e. Small Group Bible Study -- Conduct a Bible study where service is studied. You might want to purchase books about spiritual gifts that would serve as a basis for your discussions.

Stage 2

After three or four stage 1 activities, consider taking your group to the next stage. In stage 2, participants become more aware of the ministry or service environment by actually getting involved in a service project. Events that describe a stage 2 activity are one-time events that commit the individual to three or four hours of time. Examples might include:

a. Soup Kitchen -- Contact the director of a soup kitchen or homeless shelter and take the serving responsibilities for one meal.

b. Sporting Events -- Have youth take younger kids to a circus that's in town. Maybe the younger children are from your church or from a homeless shelter. It is only a one-time event that could grow to more frequent involvement.

c. Elderly Care -- Set aside one afternoon to clean up the yard of an older person in your community who is unable to do it themselves.

Stage 3

The main difference between stage 2 and stage 3 is that in the former, you are involved for only three or four hours. Stage 3, like stage 2, is a one-time event, but involves a greater time commitment. A week or more may be involved. Sample events include the following:

a. Short-Term Mission Projects -- Whether it is building a school, church, clinic, or an environmental clean-up project, short term mission endeavors increase the participant's commitment to serving others.

b. Summer Service Camp -- The Pittsburgh Project (in Pennsylvania) is set up in a way similar to a youth summer camp where you pay a fee to attend various activities. The main difference is that instead of swimming, archery and horseback riding, campers travel to inner city areas and get personally involved in tutoring, sports programs, home repair, and building relationships.

c. Documentary -- Challenge your group to document some social need or injustice. Then have the group edit the film into a half-hour documentary that can be shown at church, on TV, or to a civic or government organization.

STAGE 4

After individuals have received an intentional exposure to service through stages 1 to 3, the foundation has been laid for your group to alter their lifestyle to one of service. In stage 4 you will notice they will rearrange their lives to make serving others a major aspect of their being. They're even taking the initiative now, and some of their service activities won't even be church based! For example:

a. Park Clean Up -- A group of young people go to a park and clean up garbage because they don't have anything else to do one afternoon.

b. Summer Camp for the Handicapped -- After you trained a staff member for your Day Camp program one year, the next summer he/she volunteers to work at a State camp for the handicapped rather than at your program for pay.

c. Church Hopping -- Some of your young people miss your church services occasionally because they're taking their "adopted grandparents" to the church of their choice.

NOTE

Please be mindful of the following factors due to stage development:

- Some people in your group may already be at stage 3 or 4; others at stages 1 and 2. While you may not experience any frustration exposing a stage 3 or 4 person to ideas that are stage 1 and 2 in nature, the reverse may not be true.
- Even if you believe that many in your group are in the higher stages, use stages 1 and 2 occasionally to reinforce your previous efforts and to include newcomers that have just joined your group.
- Debriefing--Discussing, analyzing and applying the service experience helps to prepare the individual for the next stage or to affirm an already committed service lifestyle.

THE GREAT OMISSION

I t's hard to believe, we know! But few people go beyond the Great Commission when it comes time to build a foundation, even one centered on Christ. As you formulate your service plans, do some serious thinking about why your group is involved in service. Encourage discussion with your leaders and your entire group. Don't omit this important aspect in promoting a lifestyle of service. Here are two key thoughts to include in your dialogue and reflection.

1.   **Jesus did more healing than preaching**. Undoubtedly Jesus preached often, although we have a record of only one sermon--the Sermon on the Mount. However, when you survey the life of Jesus it becomes obvious that he spent much more of his time healing than preaching. Most likely, his healing gave him the right to preach (and to be heard).

The achilles heel of Christianity today is that we are heard preaching more than we are seen healing. Have you seen the bumper sticker that reads, "Christians love unborn babies more than born ones"? And we have a haunting sense that it's too true. Where did all the believers go when the young girl decided to have her baby? Where were the preaching protesters when she was kicked out of her home? Where were the people who said, "It was the right thing to do," when she used the last of her food?

Whether it's pornography, evolution, prayer in schools, "safe sex" or abortion, has the Christian community, through its healing, earned the right to be heard? If we haven't, then we aren't following the example of the One we claim to follow (and represent).

2.   **Before one can share the good news, one must become good news**. Joseph Aldrich said it this way, "Christians are to *be* good news before they *share* the good news."[1] Recognizing the frailty of our humanity, few of us would say that we are completely good news through and through. Even the most secure and mature Christan has bad days -- and even bad moments within the good days.

---

[1]Joseph Aldrich, *Life-Style Evangelism* (Portland, OR: Multnomah Press, 1981), p. 20.

But perhaps it would be better to answer the following question: When people see you coming, do they feel good about you, tolerate you, avoid you, or ignore you? If they don't perceive that you are a caring, helping person, why would they listen to your religious beliefs? Why would they want a religious experience that could do to them what apparently has been done to you? The old adage is true, "People don't care how much you know until they know how much you care." People are attracted to Jesus when they see the gospel with skin on it. When Jesus is real and the focal point of a person's life, others will be attracted to the care and acceptance demonstrated.

And so we have an enigma: Why does God choose to count on us to do so much? We also have an awesome insight into how he works-- Even in the weakness of our humanity, he can still be seen.

INDIVIDUAL GIFTEDNESS

Don't expect everyone in your group to do one activity and like it. For instance, not everyone is going to be interested in passing out literature. Don't just push *your* pet project and assume that people uninterested in it lack spiritual depth or maturity. The Holy Spirit hasn't given everyone the same gifts.

Young people are in a period of identity search. What an ideal time to expose them to a variety of service activities! Encourage them to discover, through experimentation, areas that tap into their natural interests and giftedness. This includes trying out service activities that might not have initial appeal. Give it a try to see if this is one more niche God has for you! We get to experience the joy of discovering the gifts God has given us to build up the Body of Christ through service. A few ways to determine what the individual giftedness of your group are:

- **Encourage your group to experiment.** While you may only have time to prepare one or two service ideas, facilitate the group in branching out and sampling other opportunities in which they may have an interest.
- **In a small group, go around the circle, one at a time, and have each person share a strength or talent they see in another person.** In other words, each person takes a turn describing the talents observed in Jack's life. Next, the group describes the gifts of Heather, and so on.
- **Most Christian bookstores carry books that discuss spiritual gifts at length.** Some include tests a person can take to determine their talents and gifts. Give the test to your group and then discuss ways each person can get involved according to how God has gifted them.

BEYOND YOUR COMFORT ZONE

There's tremendous risk in service. Will the recipients be glad, angry, surprised, expectant, offended, non-plussed, violent, grateful, affectionate, silent, or something else? Will you have enough resources to meet the need? Will anyone take what you have to offer? Will your safety be at risk? To what degree?

You can expect that your comfort zones will be challenged in many service activities. Our comfort zones are what's regular or normal-- what's familiar to us--to the point of being neutral. These provide security. When our environment becomes non-neutral--when things are no longer familiar to us--we find ourselves in the strange tension of danger and opportunity. The danger frightens us while the opportunity beckons to us. A non-neutral environment creates many teachable moments.

What makes an environment non-neutral? Anything different from what you usually experience. For example, taking a suburban youth group to the inner city or taking an inner city youth group to the wilderness. How about taking a group of English-speaking young people on a short-term mission trip? Or mix them with an ethnic group in America? Expose middle class North American youth to low income or upper income classes and notice how non-neutral the environment becomes.

In general, as people grow older they are more apt to avoid non-neutral environments. They'll even react strongly to get things "back to normal." That's why they tend to get into ruts. The prime time for seeking non-neutral environments is during the teen years, although young people can prefer their comfort zones, too.

Expect and invite people to enter into non-neutral environments as they become involved in service. Besides following the example of Jesus (leaving heaven to come live and die on earth was hardly neutral for Christ), non-neutral environments enhance the learning and character development of the participants. This is especially true when competent leaders help participants internalize their experience through debriefing.

DEBRIEFING

Want to really stretch the service opportunities for all they're worth? Then debrief the experience with the participants.[2] It is in the debriefing that people can reflect, question, listen, understand and apply their service activity to their lives.

Probably the most critical element in the debriefing process is the leader or facilitator. This person is an artist who guides the discussion. That's why a prescribed set of questions easily bombs and predicting exact dynamics is futile. In the flow of discussion, the basic components are:

- **Sharing what happened** ("When we fed the homeless people I was surprised that they seemed like such normal people.")
- **Drawing out people to identify the implications of their experience** ("In so many ways I'm like the homeless and they're just like me; so why do I have a home and they don't?")
- **Application and generalization** ("I'm going to see to it that the shelves of the Interfaith Food Bank are kept adequately stocked, plus I'm going to consciously resist prejudices I have against people who aren't just like me.")

Debriefing can be done during or immediatelyy following the service experience. Sometimes it's better to wait awhile so you can refer back to experiences rather than discussing it in the heat of the moment. You can even discuss an experience after it's been debriefed previously. The debriefing can take place with the group as a whole, one-on-one, or in a larger group setting that includes people who weren't even participants. It depends on what you want to develop from the service experience!

---

[2]See Steve Case, *Growing Kids: Making Your Youth Ministry Count* (Berrien Springs, MI: UTH MIN, 1989), p. 101-114.

A FEW TIPS TO REMEMBER

a. Givers and Receivers are equal in service. Don't fool yourself by thinking that if you are serving someone else you're a little better than they are. Many who serve talk about how much they *receive* as a result of *giving*. So who's giving and who's receiving? It's mutual. We need each other to give and to receive.

b. Adapt the service ideas in this book to your situation. The activities in this book are merely ideas. The needs and resources in your area will influence what you do and how much you do it. Remember the stages of service involvement, too. Are you expecting mature service lifestyles before you've even exposed your young people to a variety of service opportunities?

c. Young people can do incredible things! Don't underestimate them, and be willing to be surprised when they exceed your expectations. Remember David and Goliath? Also, Christ's disciples were in their late teens and early twenties when they were called. Recently a young person tried shooting videos of his youth group and now he's one of the major producers of Christian films. Another young person thought more people should be aware of service activities, so he started a nation-wide service awareness newspaper. Go ahead and be surprised; just don't stop them.

d. You're not the first person to serve. Sometimes people assume that since they've just come up with a service idea, they'll be the first person or group to implement it. You might barge into the office of a grocery store manager and suggest that the store donate excess or outdated supplies to a local food bank or soup kitchen. Imagine how chagrined you'd be if you then found out that the grocery store had started three different food banks in your community, and the grocery store employees staff them as volunteers!

e. Warm fuzzies aren't guaranteed. Although people often talk about how good they felt because they served, it's quite possible that the service activity you're involved with may result in hard work but not necessarily warm feelings of appreciation. In fact, you may end up feeling sour or angry. Here's a great opportunity to truly test your motivations for service. Bring on the debriefing!

Section 2: The Hands-On Service Ideas!

ADOPT
- A -
GRANDPARENT

Enrich young people by having them adopt a grandparent. The concept is for the young people to develop a relationship with a senior citizen. This requires periodic contact points and an investment of one's time, energy, and possibly finances and influence. Senior citizens can be found by checking your church directory, local retirement homes and convalescent hospitals. Work with leaders to develop the concept into a workable plan. What are the best times to get together? What are recommended activities? What kind of orientation is needed?

Here are a few potential activities:

- **Introduce Me to Your Friends -** Ask your adopted grandparent to introduce you to their friends and neighbors. Ask the friends and neighbors to tell you stories about your newly adopted grandparent.

- **Photo Share Time -** Ask your adopted grandparent to share photos of family members and places they've been. Bring some photos of your family so your adopted grandparent knows who else they're becoming related to! Have your picture taken with your adopted grandparent and send copies to relatives. Carry a copy in your wallet, too.

- **Trip to the Zoo -** Take your adopted grandparent to the zoo. Share stories about other times you've been to various zoos. Which animals do you think are the most unusual? If you could be an animal, which one would you be? What are the advantages and disadvantages to having animals caged into one location like a zoo?

- **Shopping -** Take your adopted grandparent to do some shopping *they* need to do. This might be at a mall, a local drugstore, or even a grocery store.

ADOPT - A - HIGHWAY

ou've seen the signs:

> Adopt-a-Highway
> The next two miles are cleaned by:
> Jim's Auto Sales.

Sometimes service clubs or even church groups have taken responsibility for keeping a stretch of highway clean. You can contact the government transportation department and get routed through the process to get a portion of highway with recognition for your group.

Another option is to simply clean the side of roads that aren't part of the program. You won't get the credit. What's your motivation?

Clean ups can be quite a chore if a particular roadside is really trashy. Provide plenty of heavy duty garbage bags and work in groups. Wear brightly colored clothing and keep clear of the road. If need be, have appropriate safety warnings posted so that volunteers aren't threatened by the traffic.

You may choose to adopt a particular portion of road, or simply be a clean-up crew that does spot clean ups. The same procedure could be used at parks, too.

It's good to have a few trucks in which you can deposit the filled trash bags. After dropping off your collection at the dump, clean up and go to a park for take-out pizza. (Don't litter!)

ADOPT
- AN -
ANIMAL SHELTER

Have you ever walked into a Humane Society shelter only to see the sad eyes of dogs and cats waiting for their masters? Have you ever wanted to help ease their loneliness while they wait? Here is your chance.

Contact your local Humane Society or city or county pound and explain to them that you and your group would like to take the dogs for a walk. They will point out the pooches least likely to bite. You might take along some dog bones/biscuits for extra treats. Be sure to ask the employees about the dog treat because some animals are on strict diets. Ask if they have leashes or if you should bring some rope.

Cats are more distant by nature. Do not be too aggressive with them. Stop by a store and pick up a few toys (laced with catnip) to leave with the cats. If your group wants a follow-up activity of their Humane Society trip, they can work with the Society to have a "spay or neuter your pet" emphasis or an animal adoption drive in your community.

BIG BROTHER
BIG SISTER

Frequently children, especially those in the 10-12 year-old "hero stage," are in need of positive role models. Will you be such a person for a youngster? The key element is to be a friend. To do this with a child means to be involved in their active pursuits. Most children don't want to sit around and talk. Do your talking on the run. Plan activities they would like to do. Here are a few examples:

- **Baseball Game** - If a professional baseball team isn't located nearby, perhaps a minor league game or even a community program will suffice. You might just want to play catch or a game of 3-flies-up or 500.

- **Waterslides** - While youth go to waterslides primarily to see the opposite sex, children go for the adventure of the waterslides. Can you stay with their interest rather than your own? Make sure you have lots of energy or you won't be able to keep up with them.

- **Shopping mall** - Designate a time to go to the mall. The "little brother" or "little sister" sets the agenda at the mall. You can shop or learn how to play some video games at the arcade--be prepared to get beat! Notice how differently the child views things compared to you. Note the difference in attention spans, also.

- **Make a video** - Make a short video about some of your activities or on a topic of your choice, such as strategies for squirt gun use, 25 different uses for a dictionary, how to surprise others with your niceness, etc. Take turns doing the shooting of the video as well as being the actor. Be prepared to edit as necessary. Share the video with each other's friends or at a church program.

- **Be my bud** - Would you be friends with your "little brother" or "little sister" if they were your age? Take them to a youth group activity, such as a picnic, water ski outing, group games, beach volleyball day, and have your "little brother" or "sister" be your guest. Make sure they are included and support them as a friend.

BIKES FOR TYKES

One of the most meaningful items a child will ever have is a bicycle. If you have a group that wants to get mechanical, start collecting bicycles that need minor repairs, like seat replacement, painting, or flat tire repair.

If your group doesn't want to get grease under their fingernails, visit yard sales and purchase bicycles there. You only need 10-15 dollars to purchase a bicycle in good shape. You may need to wash them up a bit. Then contact local social workers who are aware of needy children. If you give eight to ten bicycles at once to different children, think of offering a bicycle camp where you can teach them to ride their bikes safely and to fix their chain if it comes off.

BIRTHDAY MONEY TO MISSIONS

Most North Americans have lots of things they want but few things they *really* need. But when it comes time for your birthday (or Christmas or other gift-giving celebration) you're bound to receive some gifts. Rather than refusing gifts, which are symbols of thoughtfulness and support, try channeling the resources to a needy cause.

Select a project to give to, such as a missionary family or a mission school or a local soup kitchen or foster care center. Discover a manageable goal for your project, such as 30 books for the school, a tape recorder and collection of tapes for the missionary, silverware for 200 for the soup kitchen, etc.

Notify those who are likely to give you a gift regarding your project that you're directing all your resources to a particular cause at this time--in fact to the point of preferring cash gifts or "in kind" donations to your cause. Be careful not to come across as soliciting gifts (unless you're doing fund raising!) or as "holier-than-thou" for having such a project.

Those who give to your cause should be thanked and notified of how their donation was utilized. When you make your cumulative gift, be sure to mention that it really is from a host of people, not just you. Be another cog in the wheel of "receiving in order to give."

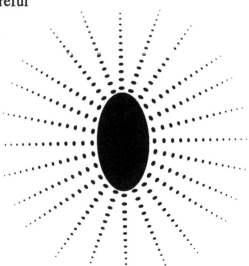

BIRTHDAY PARTIES

Shelters for families and single parents have plenty of needs. One meaningful activity for everyone is to sponsor a monthly birthday party for the children of these shelters. Frequently their families do not have the money to have birthday parties for their children.

Grocery stores will often donate cakes and ice cream. Toy stores are also receptive to providing gifts for children, or you can collect toys by conducting community toy drives.

Contact the director of the shelter and arrange for an appropriate time. You can either go once or make it a monthly event. Plan on about an hour-and-a-half to two hours, leaving you time for the party, clean up and establishing some relationships.

BIRTHDAYS

It means a lot to members in a congregation when people remember their birthday. Here are a couple of ideas on ways you can get the word out about birthdays.

First, volunteer to provide a bulletin board that features the birthdays of members for each month. In January, you could cut out snow flakes and write the person's name on it and the birthday. February could be hearts (Valentine's Day); March - shamrocks; October - leaves or pumpkins, etc.

Secondly, you could type up a list of birthdays in chronological order and have enough copies printed to distribute to each family. Many churches are small enough to fit everyone on a page or two. Encourage members to place the list on the inside of a frequently used cupboard door so they will see it often. Also suggest that everyone have a special prayer for their fellow members when it is their birthday.

Note: When you list the birth date, do not include the year they were born. Many people could be offended if you do. A simple list of day and month will suffice.

BLOOD BANK

One of the amazing things about the bodies God made for us is that the blood that nourishes a person can be given to nourish another person. The Bible says that the life is in the blood. Blood donors are real life givers.

Although blood donation is sometimes thought of in emergency situations in which somebody is in need of lots of blood or they have a rare blood type, blood banks are usually in need of more donors.

While the Red Cross may set up mobile blood bank clinics at malls or fairs, commercial blood banks accept donated blood and distribute it to area hospitals. This usually requires an appointment that includes a medical history, a blood check and possibly a physical examination by a physician they provide. Check the yellow pages in your local phone book and look under "blood bank."

Drawing the blood itself usually takes less than 10 minutes. The same person can donate blood every two months. Most blood banks don't pay the donors for their blood. They consider it a donation. A few pass on $10-$20 to the donor. You may choose to utilize the funds for another service activity.

There are other options than simply donating the blood. Some people donate the platelets in their blood. They can do this every two weeks (rather than every two months for blood). The process takes two hours rather than 10 minutes. Another option is to donate blood plasma. This can be done every three days and takes 45-60 minutes.

 # **10** BREAD BAKING AND DISTRIBUTION

So often churches expect people in the community to come to the church for services, or they ask people in the community for things (some even solicit cash donations door-to-door). Perhaps it's time to turn the tables and go to the community and give them something--no strings attached.

Get a group together to bake small loaves of bread. This can be done in several houses or as a large group at the church (if you have the necessary kitchen facilities and equipment there). Baking the bread can be loads of fun, especially if it's a new experience for many.

Once you have enough loaves of bread to go into the community, get ready for some surprises. You'll probably need to have a brief note of explanation to identify the source of the bread, such as "The youth from Encino Avenue Church hope this bread brings you the spirit of joy we love to share."

Leave a loaf of bread for the people you are able to meet as you go door-to-door in your community. Some may expect that you are selling it. Others will try to donate to your group. Gently point out that your purpose in doing this bread distribution is just to share with others, not to get anything from them. If people insist, take their donation and tell them it will go into the youth fund at your church. Your purpose is not to put guilt on people or make them "owe you" something. The purpose is just to share with them. You will be amazed at the reactions to such "disinterested benevolence."

BOX CITY

Misunderstandings about homelessness abound. Even the total number of homeless individuals is hotly debated (estimates vary from 250,000 to as high as 7,000,000 depending on how you define homelessness).

With Box City, individuals are invited to spend the night sleeping in a cardboard box, in a parking lot, or alley way, simulating a homeless experience. In the morning, a meal similar to those offered by soup kitchens is provided. The meal is followed by a tour of local homeless and runaway shelters showing specific organizations in which Box City participants can become involved within their communities. After the tour, debriefing groups are formed to help further internalize what has been learned.

Start the event after supper on a Friday or Saturday night. Try to conclude by noon the following day. Do your homeless people get lunch or do they have to fend for themselves?

Note: A Box City how-to kit is now available and includes a Box City organizer, program helps, site selection, menu, debriefing questions, suggested tour schedule, promotional hints, follow-up and much more. To order the kit, call Youth and Young Adult Ministries Consultants at their toll-free number, 1-800-440-1670. Cost: $10.

BULLETIN BOARD

Bulletin boards offer public information. Some are rather drab, others are in need of repair, and still others are simply out of date. Sometimes there is a need for a bulletin board in a public setting, but nobody has provided one or contacted an owner or manager to see if one can be set up.

Two major factors to consider when putting up a bulletin board are:

* What do we want to communicate through the bulletin board?
* Where will the bulletin board be?

If you want to communicate a religious thought or concept, or promote a religious activity or event, the bulletin board will need to be in a location that permits religious material. Is it in a place your target group will see it, or are you just putting it up for whomever happens to come by?

Other topics besides overtly religious material include health, safety, family, cooperation, recreation, responsibility, service, value of people, respect for people and property, positive role models and patriotism.

Locations for bulletin boards include schools, grocery stores, laundromats, churches, recreation centers, clubs, bus stations, airports, strip malls, fast food stores, retirement homes, pizza places, business centers, child care centers, apartment house complexes, and anywhere else you think of.

A craft or paper store will have plenty of bulletin board materials. You can also get by with a variety store such as K-Mart or Wal-Mart. Get your concept together and then work your creativity into the space you have available. You might even be able to do a series of bulletin boards over time.

CARENET

Do you remember how your mom took care of you when you were sick as a child? Who provides that tender loving care to people who get sick today--people like single moms, the elderly, singles and those without relatives in town? Carenet may be one of the most meaningful services you could provide for your community!

First, set up a council of four or five people, with one functioning as the chairperson. They activate the Carenet when someone calls to inform them about a person who is sick. Volunteers are then set in motion. (Some of your best volunteers will be those who have been on the receiving end of Carenet.)

Second, volunteers who specialize in cooking meals, washing clothes and watching children, descend on the home of the sick person. By this time the council has appointed a lead person to coordinate care for the person. That lead person can recruit others to assist.

Third, the lead person reports back to the council, giving updates and indicating the status of needs in relationship to available volunteers. As volunteers complete their tasks with an individual, they are then available to serve others in the network called Carenet. Watch out, because Carenet may soon permeate your entire community with a powerful presence for God!

HANDS

CHILD CARE

Most parents are in need of child care at various times. Some don't have the luxury of family members nearby to care for their little ones. Some don't have the convenience of baby sitters they can trust or ones they can afford. Here's an opportunity for other members of the Church to function as family. Provide child care at select times or for specific groups.

Be sure a competent leader oversees the child care. Many teens can assist, especially if they have some experience at baby sitting. Activities can include playing games, reading books, drawing or making other crafts, listening to stories and recreational games. Be prepared to divide the group by age categories if a lot of children are present. You might need to set limits on the number of children based on the number of care givers.

This service might be for a short time period, such as two or three nights during the Christmas season so parents can go Christmas shopping or be in the annual Church Christmas pageant.

The child care service might also be of an on-going nature, such as each Thursday evening for "Couple's Night Out" or for single parents to follow up job leads or to attend night classes.

One option is to have the child care personnel take care of the children in the children's own homes instead of at the church, especially if it's in the evening and they need to be put to bed. With such an arrangement, plans will need to be made in advance to coordinate people, schedules and transportation. A central clearinghouse such as the church office or a well-run voice mail can be used for volunteers and for parents to get together.

CHILD TUTORING SERVICES

ith many parents gone until early evening, a lot of kids are "home alone" after school. Begin a tutoring service for kids in your neighborhood once or twice a week. Start after school and go for an hour to an hour-and-a-half. Make sure that you obtain written permission from the child's parent/guardian.

If the students are having trouble in classes you are weak in, recruit some extra help. Invite community educators to assist you. Remember to start simple. Offer tutoring in math, English or reading.

Local schools or churches may let you use their facilities to hold your tutoring sessions. Keep your class size small - maybe three to four students per tutor.

Note: Many church insurance companies are requiring a background check on volunteers. This is done through the FBI. Cost is approximately $40. If your church does not have that information, contact your local police department.

CHILDREN'S CHURCH

Most church services are geared for adults. Most churches don't have a relevant worship service for children. Some churches provide nursery care. But what about those who are 6-10 years of age? Is worship for them simply a matter of "sit down, shut up and color in your book"?

A separate children's church can give them a meaningful, age-appropriate worship experience. It also gives young people an opportunity to lead in church and to serve others. You'll need vivacious leaders, a person or two with some musical talents, and other helpers to sit among the kids for crowd control.

Children's church has the same components as an adult service, but it's geared for kids. For example, instead of just reading some announcements from the front, have puppets spread the word to each other. Instead of just reading a passage of Scripture, have kids take turns sharing "Good News" from the past week. Instead of a sermon, have a skit that gives the biblical message.

Children's Church Curriculum:
    Skituations
    (800) 322-1336

    Critter County
    Loveland Communications
    (513) 677-1999

CHILDREN'S HOSPITAL VISITATION

ost good sized communities have a hospital that specializes in children's care. If there is no kid's hospital in your area, your hospital probably does have a children's wing. In many instances, youth up to 18 years of age are included in these areas.

Personal visitation is always a meaningful activity. Consider combining it with other fun activities such as a clown ministry, drama team or musical group. Balloons with helium are always a big hit. Special tanks filled with helium are available at most large stores that sell party equipment. This activity is great for a one-time event or every-month type of outreach. Young people in hospitals really appreciate visitors who help to break the monotony of hospitalization. (See "Clowning")

CHILDREN'S RELIGIOUS EDUCATION PROGRAMS

ometimes extra help is needed for children's religious education programs, such as Vacation Bible School, Neighborhood Bible Club, etc. But there are times when the regular religious education program needs volunteers, too.

Sometimes it's a person who can play the piano. Other times it's a need for an animated story teller. Would you be willing to bring some bunny rabbits or a baby goat for the children to pet? Can you use puppets or twist balloons into animals or do a few basic magic tricks? How about serving as a greeter or a small group teacher on a regular basis? Would you be willing to substitute on occasion?

Younger children will frequently have the same program week after week for 3-6 months. When the program changes, it includes lots of props and other decorations, as well as support supplies that might require a concerted thrust to get it all together. Do you have skills, creativity and/or patience to help?

Just as some people are gifted to work with older people and others have special abilities with young people, there are likely to be some people in your youth group (maybe you!) who are gifted to work with children. Not everyone has the gift, but it's worth experimenting to find out if you do. Some children's religious education programs are very elaborate and most could use some additional help.

19

CHRISTMAS PACKAGES FOR PRISONERS

ontact the local prison about your desire to provide Christmas packages for prisoners who have no family or friends. They will give you instructions on how to package the gifts so that their security remains intact.

You can place in each package an assortment of candy, magazines or books. Socks and underwear are also welcomed. You can ask prison officials what inmates can and cannot receive in the mail.

If your group wants to do something on a regular basis, contact the prison officials and obtain a list of birthdays and provide birthday presents for the prisoners. Do not forget to vary the gifts from year to year, or person to person. Your good intentions could be misunderstood if you send the same thing each time. It can come across as very impersonal.

CHURCH CLEAN UP

Church janitors are some of the least appreciated people around. Few notice when they do a good job. When they mess up, everyone seems to know.

Contact your pastor with the news that your group wants to give the janitor a break. Find out when the cleaning is normally done (usually once a week). If cleaning takes place on Friday, arrange to come in Thursday night. Obtain a copy of the job description from the pastor or church secretary and make appropriate cleaning assignments within your group. Also take advantage of the job description to make a list of the equipment you will need to do the job right.

Then, write the janitor a thank you letter for all that's done each week and include a list of the tasks your group did. It is possible that all of the janitor's duties are not listed on the job description. By sharing the things your group did accomplish, you ensure that the janitor will not get in trouble for having missed something.

Lastly, if the janitor is paid, make sure payment is received this week, too (even though your group did the cleaning). Some janitors count on these wages to supplement their income.

CHURCH FACILITIES AVAILABLE

t's amazing how few hours each week churches are used. Consider making available space in your church for the following programs:

- Allow non-profit humanitarian agencies to set up their offices in rooms that are hardly used. Let them use your church phone number as their number. This service will breathe new life into your phone and your church by making it a center of people activity.
- If you're located near a college, pay high school students to babysit for single parents who are students. Offer the service from 7-9 PM, Monday through Thursday. Babysitting can take place in one of the classrooms, and a fellowship hall can be converted into a study hall. Consider offering extended hours during mid-terms and finals.
- If you have a gym or playing field, offer the city the use of your facility for their recreation program. If there is no recreation program, start one and host it.
- Construct low-cost housing on vacant church-owned land that produces rental income and helps meet area housing shortages.

CHURCH OFFICE ASSISTANCE

Many church offices rely completely on volunteers for services. Some might have a part-time secretary, but that's it. Those that have a full-time secretary usually could still use more help.

Some of the extra tasks involve mailouts for special church news or services, a monthly newsletter, weekly bulletins that need to be stuffed with various inserts, etc. Sometimes it's a tremendous release to just answer the phone(s) so the multi-purpose secretary, receptionist, administrative assistant can do the regular tasks.

These are the kinds of services that can be a one-shot activity, especially in an emergency or for a one-time task. They could easily be a regular service activity, such as running visitor follow up letters for the pastor to sign after each weekend.

It may be a matter of just 30-60 minutes each week, but it can make a much bigger difference in the efficiency and spirit of the church office. And it serves as a reminder that it is *your* church--so help carry your part of the load!

CHURCH SERVICE

Some churches set aside one church service each year for a special youth emphasis day. They may turn over the entire program to the young people. Have the youth do the preaching and make sure they've been coached. You may prefer to have the sermon delivered in three parts by three youth presenters (ideal for a 3-point sermon).

Other components of the worship service, such as group singing, congregational prayer, offering, children's story, and even announcements should take on a more youthful flair rather than having the young people simply impersonate adults.

Talk this through with the young people. Help them realize that while they might not want to be as outlandish as they could be with a completely youth congregation, they still need to be true to what their convictions and worship expressions are. There should be some expectation that when the youth conduct the worship service it won't be too conventional or traditional! Make sure there is purpose to what you do, the people have adequate preparation and instruction for worshipping, and expect some criticism from those who want things "the way they've always been." If they don't react, you probably didn't do what you should have done!

Don't limit the youth involvement to once a year. Make arrangements for them to lead in other components at other times, too. A young person can give the children's story, or the drama group can illustrate one of the pastor's points in her sermon, or young people can do the special music or be part of the band or singers who lead in congregational singing. It's their church, too!

The same component, or parts of it, can be shared with other churches or youth groups, perhaps on an exchange basis.

CLEAN WINDSHIELDS

Provide a windshield cleaning service in a parking lot. If you're going to clean someone's windshield, especially if it's done as a surprise while they're away from their car, make sure you do a quality job. Here are a few tips:

- Use enough cleaner to wet the window rather than leaving smear marks
- Don't let excess cleaner run down the hood or side of the car--it leaves a dirt streak
- Spray or wipe cleaner directly on the window. Don't let overspray get on other parts of the car, giving it a splattered look
- Use clean cloths; otherwise you're just sharing dirt
- Wipe the windshield dry; wet windshields attract more dirt
- When you clean side mirrors, try not to move them--it can be annoying to have to readjust them
- If the windshield already is clean, leave it alone

You may want to leave a brief note under the windshield wiper explaining what happened. It can be a short, friendly note, such as:

The youth from First Church are seeing things more clearly now. We hope you do, too, after this complimentary windshield cleaning.
OR
Windshield cleaning compliments of Park Avenue Church.
OR
What's this? A windshield cleaning by the youth at the Christian Connection. Come check us out Saturday nights at 8:00 at the corner of El Camino and Bradshaw.

CLOWNING

You may know some people who always seem to be clowning around. Use that "gift" to bring joy into the lives of others. Some people you might not consider to be clown-like might take on a new aura once they get dressed up and glob on enough make-up to protect their original identity.

Most Christian bookstores will have materials on how to do clown ministry. Costume stores carry colorful wigs, appropriate clothing and clown make-up. You can also adapt things for less money and a little creativity--such as slitting a hole in a hollow plastic red ball for a clown nose rather than purchasing an "actual" clown nose.

Learning how to twist balloons into animal shapes can be learned in a short time. A few magic tricks can also bring lots of glee, too. If you move from one place to another with just brief stops, you can repeat your few tricks many times with no trouble at all (provided you don't have some groupies trailing you. If you do, they will quickly get bored of watching you do the same four things!) If you are going to be clowning for a long period in one place, you will need to have a much larger repertoire.

Now it's time to find some people who need a little cheering up. Look for gatherings of children in one place, such as preschools or elementary schools, foster care homes, playgrounds or parks, pediatric wards in hospitals, Vacation Bible School, and even parties. Don't limit yourself just to gatherings of children. Surprise people at an office, outside (or inside) a restaurant during lunch hour, on a street corner, in a parade, between innings during a little league game, a physician's or dentist's office, or anywhere else people are.

A terrific little book about clowning is *Clown Ministry* by Floyd Shaffer. It's available for $10.99 from Group. Call 1-800-447-1070 to order it.

26

COACH

o doubt you have some real jocks in your group who are patient and explain things well. Encourage them to coach a baseball, basketball, soccer, swimming, gymnastics or track team for their community. In many areas, kids are turned away because adequate coaching is unavailable. It may seem like a big commitment, but seasons commonly last only eight to ten weeks.

An awesome way to establish meaningful friendships is through the relationships you form with the team and their parents. Now more than ever, kids need individuals who are willing to spend quality time with them. Why not try coaching? Do it with your friends!

COMMUNITY SERVICE HOURS

Most city councils or county commissioner meetings have a space in their agenda for new business. The chairperson will ask those in attendance if there is new business. Anyone can respond at this point. Take your group to the meeting and offer them 200 hours of community service on projects determined by the council during the new business time. With a group of 25 working an eight hour shift, you can fulfill your commitment.

If they're too shocked to know what to come up with, you might suggest projects such as painting public buildings, cleaning a community park, or volunteering at your community visitor bureau.

Remember that some councils like new business submitted in writing. A quick phone call to City Hall or the Commissioner's office will inform you as to the requirements you will need to meet.

COMMUNITY SURVEYS

Many churches have developed a reputation for being issue oriented. Right-to-life, creation, prayer in school and many other issues have defined the "message" these churches send out.

Are these the issues, however, that the people in your community face everyday? Probably not, though some do. Why not survey the people in your community to find out the issues that challenge them. One church learned that families in their community were having financial difficulties, which led to marital problems and strained relationships with their children.

Survey as many homes as you can, then take the results to your pastor or church board. If your group sees a need they are interested in responding to, go for it! If you see needs that can be met by your congregation, encourage them to become more active in the community. Take them along with you on your projects.

CPR CLASS

Thousands of lives could be saved each year if everyone knew basic CPR skills. Why not sponsor a class with your youth group and invite your congregation and community. In just a few hours, participants will be equipped with the skills necessary to save lives.

Certified instructors in CPR can be found in many places. Contact your local Red Cross, ambulance service, police or fire department and hospitals for qualified professional instructors. Certification is available to all who successfully complete the course.

Another class you might offer is the certified first-aid course that adds a multiplicity of life saving skills to each participant's abilities.

Sponsor a class every year for you, your congregation and your community.

DAY CAMP

uring summer vacation lots of children have nothing to do but watch television reruns. And teens are in need of jobs. Why not employ the teens to conduct a summer Day Camp for children in your community? Because many kids come from single parent homes or dual income families, a number of parents are looking for supervised activities during times their children are on vacation but the parents aren't.

Some places have sophisticated and expensive summer programs with highly trained staff. Others cater to those unable to pay a lot, and still others offer something for those who have virtually nothing. The type of children you're reaching and the amount you're able to charge in fees or raise with donations will impact the activities and staff for your Day Camp.

Don't view the Day Camp as merely an employment opportunity for the youth. Use this as leadership training for them as well. Staff training can begin before the actual start of Day Camp, and it can continue with daily staff training/worship periods. You'll need regular points of contact for your staff to deal with the issues at hand in addition to shaping their leadership through these real-life experiences.

Some Day Camps utilize readily available resources such as community swimming pools, bowling alleys, water slides, amusement parks, zoos, parks and recreation areas. The staff members function as counselors. In many instances it's wise to group your campers by age category and sometimes by gender.

A weekly schedule might include swimming lessons, field trips to candy factories or bakeries, bowling, rafting, putt-putt golf and water slides. Some Day Camps teach skills in areas such as team sports, ceramics, skateboarding, small engines, gymnastics, arts and crafts, swimming and even tennis.

DISASTER RESPONSE TEAM (DART)

Every year your local paper is filled with disasters that have impacted the lives of individuals and families. For most people, the majority of these life-changing experiences go unnoticed.

DaRT teams are designed to provide a specific response to these often forgotten hurting people. Assign a person or persons to "scan" your daily or weekly local papers for individuals or families who have lost a family member or a home to fire. Just check the local section of the newspaper. Car accidents and job lay-offs are other incidents to watch for. If there are too many for your group to respond to, select an area more manageable (1/2 mile radius of your church or organization).

Once an individual or family has been identified, the scanner(s) notifies a team of individuals who determine what the appropriate response should be. If a fire has destroyed a home, the victim may need clothing, food and shelter (10% of all homeless families are homeless because their home burned down, and housing shortages rob them of a replacement home).

In the case of a lost loved one, visits from trained grief counselors and your support staff can meet real needs by offering meals, lawn mowing, support, etc. The type and number of responses your group is involved in is up to you.

After your initial contact, appoint a person from your team to follow up every two weeks or as reason dictates, to determine if further needs can be met.

DRAMA GROUP

ne way to make a message really come to life is to put it into the form of a skit, pantomime, play or other form of drama. While a few extroverts might come across as natural actors who can "ham it up" most people need some practice and coaching to really pull off some worthwhile drama. Frequently one key leader is all that is needed to spearhead a drama group. But the rest of the members must demonstrate commitment, too.

Drama not only communicates to the observer(s), but the participants are affected by it, too. As young people experiment with different identities during adolescence, drama provides one avenue to do so for brief periods of time without long-term consequences. Some people who seem shy might be able to really blossom by "acting" in other roles.

A drama group must have opportunities to perform or it will stagnate. Volunteer to do a skit for your youth group or some of the children's classrooms for their religious education time. Do health or human relationships skits for public schools. Be a street artist and do your drama on a street corner, plaza, or other gathering place for amateurs.

A number of sources exist for drama material. One that is highly respected for Christian material is Lillenas Publishing, which has lots of dramas and even a newsletter. Contact them at:

Lillenas Publishing
P. O. Box 419527
Kansas City, MO 64141
Phone: 800-877-0700

ENCOURAGE A POLITICIAN

very election that comes and goes leaves a trail of beat-up egos and hurt people. You may even be happy that some candidate or incumbent is not elected. Think about how his/her family might feel. What will they do now? Where will they live? Not all politicians have golden parachutes.

Below, find a few ways you can cheer up the losers of election day:

- Send flowers
- Go out and buy donuts and drop them off at their staff's office.
- Fax them a kind note thanking them for what they did accomplish. You might even make special reference to a law or project that was a result of their efforts.
- Send a letter signed by everyone in your group wishing them the best in the future.

34 ENVIRONMENTAL AWARENESS

Here's one way to promote an awareness of environmentalism from the perspective of glorifying God. For each day of creation week, do an activity that honors and/or brings joy based on what was created on that day (see Genesis 1:1 - 2:3 if you don't remember).

1st day - LIGHT - Spend one hour wearing a blindfold. What would life be like without light? Visit a blind person and ask for their perspective on life. What are they "in the light" about where you're still "in the dark" in comparison?

2nd day - AIR - Exercise to increase your oxygen intake. Ride your bike or walk instead of driving your car (reduce pollutants). Try hang gliding or ride in a glider.

3rd day - LAND, PLANTS - Experiment with different spices and herbs to season your food. Plant some seeds. Clean up garbage at a park or along a road.

4th day - SUN, MOON, STARS - Go to a planetarium. Read a book about stars. Take a romantic walk in the moonlight with a special friend.

5th day - FISH, BIRDS - Visit an aquarium or go fishing to feed the fish rather than catching them for your own food. Buy or make a bird feeder and stock it with bird seed.

6th day - ANIMALS, HUMANS - Take a trip to the zoo. If you were Adam, what names would you have given to the different animals you see? Eat vegetarian today.

7th day - SABBATH - The birthday of the world, so have a party! It's a day to make different from every other day of the week. Use this time for things that you'd never do on other days: phone somebody you didn't have time for this past week, arrange pictures into a family photo album, go white water rafting to appreciate God's creation, meditate with your Creator and be reminded of who you are (your identity) based on God's view of you, conduct a worship service in honor of God.

35 ENVIRONMENTAL PRESERVATION

Lots can be done to preserve or actually restore the environment. Plant a tree, start a recycling program, include ecology as part of your short-term mission trip (contact Maranatha Volunteers International at 916-920-1900 for more information), buy an acre of rain forest (call 408-441-1571 for more information).

You can also gear your purchases of goods to environmentally friendly products. Ask yourself: What had to die for me to purchase this? North Americans ravage the environment with much of our packaging of goods. Jot a note to the company and tell them why you purchased their product, or send a note to a company whose product you didn't purchase and tell them why.

The Christian Environmental Association (CEA) was started to call Christians to love God, serve people and care for creation. Membership is $25 per year and provides the members with a monthly newsletter and discounts on all CEA products and services. Write to CEA at 1650 Zanker Road, Suite 150, San Jose, CA 95112 or call 408-441-1571.

You or other members of your group probably have several ideas or activities you've already participated in for the environment. For more ideas of what you can do to preserve the environment, Tony Campolo and Gordon Aeschliman have written a book entitled *50 Ways You Can Help Save the Planet*. It's available from CEA.

FAMILY, GROUP PHOTOS

 uy a polaroid camera and some film and hang out at a community park and offer to take family/group photos at no charge. One minute later - shazam! the photo is then presented to the family or group.

The strength of this idea is that it is so simple anyone can do it, and it does not require any training.

Remember to introduce yourself, "we are from such-and-such church or school," and then ask if you can take their photograph.

37 FAMILY WORSHIP BY YOU

When children are born into a family, frequently the parents feel an urge to become involved in a local church, especially for the training of their child(ren). By the time adolescence comes around, many teens express a disinterest in church, and perhaps their families as well.

Take the offensive. It certainly will be a challenge. Have a family time for a group worship experience. The adolescent can initiate the gathering and lead in the activity. It can be short and simple, such as a discussion about current events and how they relate (or don't relate) to spiritual things. Have family members act out one of the parables or stories of Jesus. Find a proverb or two (from the book of Proverbs--in the Bible after Psalms) and ask other members of the family to comment on whether or not they have found this to be a proverb in their lives. You could sing a song or have a prayer circle.

Perhaps the major obstacle will be to work out a 5-10 minute block of time for the whole family. For those who are fearful they can't think of anything to do for a family worship time, consider these resources:

Worship Ideas Newsletter
Steve Case
Carmichael, CA: Piece of the Pie Ministries
Call 916-944-3928 to order a subscription

10-Minute Devotions for Youth Groups (in 3 volumes)
Loveland, CO: Group, 1989, 1992, 1993
ISBN 0-931529-85-9; 1-55945-068-1; 1-55945-171-8

The Family Devotions Idea Book
Evelyn Blitchington
Minneapolis, MN: Bethany House, 1982
ISBN 0-87123-254-5

FEED THE HOMELESS

One of the most popular service activities for many young people is to feed the homeless. The level of commitment and resources needed vary tremendously. Most soup kitchens have a rather modest beginning, with a few volunteers and a somewhat temporary system of supplying food. Many individuals and groups find it more manageable to join forces with an established soup kitchen, perhaps providing human resources for preparing, serving and cleaning up one day a month. The activity many want to experience is some actual contact with the homeless people, rather than only working behind the scenes.

Another way to help might be to solicit food for the soup kitchen's food bank, or sort through and clean what has been donated, or provide delivery service to get donated items from their source to the soup kitchen.

Some homeless feeding programs require that people "pay" for their meal by first sitting through a religious service of singing and preaching before they receive their free meal. Can you provide musicians and preachers in addition to food service people?

You can also take the very direct approach and deliver food to the "homes" of homeless people. Where do they live? Usually under bridges, in parks, by rivers, in fields around warehouses, etc. Ask local police, soup kitchen personnel, or the homeless people themselves.

Plan to have opportunities for lively discussion with your young people after your experience. Why don't homeless people do something about their situation? Why don't they show more appreciation for what we do for them? Would I ever come to a soup kitchen if I were hungry? What do I have that they don't have? What do they have that I'm missing? Should we become involved in trying to help the homeless obtain shelter? Should we try to help them get jobs? Besides my recent service, what will I do in the future for the homeless?

39 FOOD CLOSET- STAFFING

Your church or other community service center may have a food closet they use for food distribution on a daily, weekly or as-food-is-available basis. See if you can assist in the food distribution.

Those who come for food might come alone or as a family. Be prepared to have a variety of quantities. Typically food closets stock non-perishable food items, such as canned soups, vegetables and fruits; dry goods such as rice, beans, pasta, and cereal. You'll want to be able to put together a box or bag of food that makes a complete meal or two. What will you do when they ask for silverware, plates, bowls and cups, a can opener? What if they need pots and pans? How about a stove?

Will you also have articles of clothing, blankets, toiletries? Will you have references for them if they need free shelter or soup kitchens for hot meals? Will you have bus coupons for them to get from your place to another food stop? Can you connect them with job opportunities if they're looking for some?

Be aware of the need and opportunity to debrief the various interactions. How do you discern between the needy and the greedy? What if the people complain about the food you're giving to them? Would you be grateful if this food were given to you? How would you respond if you found out some of the people sold their food to others and used the money for booze? Why did the people spend their entire monthly government check the first week? What if the people receiving food drive away in a fancy car? What can you do about those who want to receive handouts, but aren't interested in working? Would you ever come to a food closet to receive food?

FOOD CLOSET-STOCKING

In order for a food closet to provide food, it must have food. Sometimes food closets have regular sources of food. Others may get dried foods, but they may lack canned goods. Others might be short on tableware.

During Thanksgiving and Christmas, a number of people think about the need to provide food for others. But what about during February, May or August?

Here are a few ways to fill some empty shelves at a food closet:

- Set up box collections in your church foyer and publicize it to the congregation. You might want to kick it off by making it part of the church service and call it "Thanksgiving in April."
- Telephone church members and solicit food closet items for them to bring to church this coming weekend.
- Go door-to-door and ask for food closet items. Include a flyer that describes the services of the food closet and how others can be involved, including how they can contribute in the future.
- Distribute large, empty, brown grocery bags door-to-door with a sheet of paper describing what your group is doing and why. Ask for the house occupants to put in the bag whatever items they'd like to donate to the food closet. They can set the bag outside their front door on a given date (1-3 days after the day the bags are distributed) and your group will come back through the area to collect and deliver them to the food closet.
- After getting permission from a grocery store manager, set up a food closet booth outside the store and ask patrons to purchase an extra item during their shopping trip that they can add to the food closet collection on their way out of the store.

41 FOOD MERCHANTS TO FOOD BANKS

Government and self-imposed regulations force food merchants to throw away food after it's been on their shelves for a certain period of time. Frequently the food is still edible, especially if it is used within a short period of time. Some already donate these food items to food banks or soup kitchens. But some haven't gotten around to it or don't know whom to contact.

You can serve as the catalyst for this connection to occur, or perhaps be pleasantly surprised to find out how many companies already are involved in something like it. You may be needed to deliver the food for some of the groups.

Examples of food merchants include grocery stores, distributors of bread, chips, canned foods, meats, produce and frozen foods. You can also contact bakeries, delis, fast food outlets, restaurants, donut shops, candy stores and food processing plants.

Food banks can be located by checking the yellow pages of your phone directory or by asking local churches or government officials. If things are already happening, you may choose to simply get involved in existing programs that might need additional volunteer help.

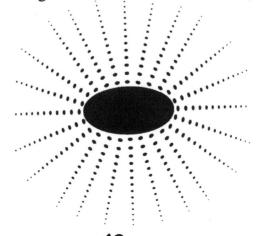

FREE CAR WASH

 btain permission from a store that is willing to let you use part of their parking lot to hold a free car wash and give the store the credit! Have volunteers from your group stand by the road with free car wash signs. The signs will increase the store's business as the people shop while their cars are being washed.

Make sure the group does a good job on the cars. You are trying to do the store a favor, not give them a bad reputation. Rinse the cars first and then wash them carefully. Have two people, one on each side, vacuum each car with shopvacs.

You will need hoses, buckets, soap, sponges or washcloths, lots of towels, cardboard (for the signs) and trash bags for garbage.

FRESHMEN ORIENTATION

College freshmen frequently need more help than the basic orientation offered by most schools. Here are some ways you can help make it an easier transition time for freshmen.

- **Registration -** many schools have a separate registration time for first year students. Become familiar with the registration process and then hang out during registration time looking for the lost and confused (they are easy to spot!) and try to assist them in whatever way you can.
- **Many schools have bookstores that offer textbooks at greatly reduced costs.** If the store is not well known, pass out information sheets telling where the store is. If your school doesn't have one, start one. What a golden opportunity for a business entrepreneur (not just a business major)! Quality used textbooks will always be needed.
- **Put together a page or two information sheet** that informs freshmen about the various, yet little known, services offered around the campus such as the location of the tutoring center, employment bulletin board, cheap eats, etc., and pass it out during registration.

WE ARE

HIS

HANDS

FUN RUN

A great way to raise the awareness concerning healthful living or other issues is by sponsoring a Fun Run of five to ten kilometers (5K=3.1 miles; 10K=6.2 miles). Contact local newspapers, TV and radio stations to have public service announcements made about the event.

Contact local businesses and health care providers for prizes and awards. Also, charge each participant a $10 entry fee and provide them with either a hat (cost about $4) or T-shirt (cost about $5). Proceeds can be donated to a public health program, child abuse prevention agency, homeless shelter or many other worthy programs.

You'll need many volunteers to pull off the event. You will need people to register runners, collect money, some will need to be stationed along the route that has been approved by the local police. Volunteer Emergency Medical Technicians (EMTs) are a good idea if runners are injured or overcome by heat exhaustion. A Walkie-talkie system will help keep volunteers in touch with each other. A local Radio Shack or other business may donate these for shared sponsorship. A large group of volunteers will be needed at the finish line. A group for recording times of finishers is a good idea along with a group to care for the exhausted.

At the awards ceremony, have a guest speaker give an 8-10 minute address to draw attention to the topic or theme behind your Fun Run. Be sure to thank your co-sponsors and the community for their support. Each year you sponsor the event, it should grow. Don't be discouraged by a low turnout one year. Keep improving your plan and word will get around.

GIFT WRAPPING

Here is an event that can involve everyone. Challenge every family to buy two rolls of wrapping paper, a bag of bows or ribbons and a roll of scotch tape and take them to the front of the church the weekend before and after Thanksgiving.

Contact a local mall or store for permission to set up your free service. Your group can get all of its shopping done early, avoid the long lines at the register and free up those last few days for staffing the gift-wrapping service. Most people buy a majority of their purchases the two or three days before Christmas.

This service can mean a lot to the rushed. While they wait, serve free cookies and a drink.

Place a large banner offering your service behind your table. You can also mention the name of your group. If your church is hosting a special Christmas program, hand out a flier about it, or compile a list of various Christmas programs in the community.

HANDS

GRAFFITI CLEANUP

raffiti is an eyesore for everyone in the community. Whether they are schools, businesses or homes, nothing is sacred to the vandal. Gangs stake-out their territory using their signature. Others just randomly select sites and do their thing.

Many groups have had positive experiences in curbing graffiti activity. Try one or both of the ideas listed below:

- Adopt-a-wall (building). Have your group, once a week, for as long as needed, paint over fresh graffiti. If you are in it for the long run, you will win out. If you give up after a couple of weeks, you'll be laughed at. Therefore, seriously consider your commitment to the project. If you're in, go for it. If you're not sure, stay out and put up with graffiti.
- Sponsor a mural contest where local artists are assigned certain walls to paint (local artists will have better reception from the community than outsiders). Make sure you get the owner's permission or your contest could be misunderstood as graffiti. Contact local businesses to donate prizes and select an impartial

panel to judge the winners. You can receive some great media attention for this. Take advantage of it and get the word out about graffiti busters. Some communities have learned that when they use local artists, the local youth tend not to vandalize the murals because the artist is seen as one of their own.

GREETERS AT CHURCH

Most churches have some people designated as official greeters. Their task is to give a welcome to both members and visitors as they arrive. Some are very aggressive; others are sensitive to the fact that some people prefer a low-key welcome rather than a fanfare.

While most churches have official greeters, few of them include young people in their cadre of volunteer greeting staff. Have some of the sanguine people in your youth group be part of the welcoming team (not just for the youth group meeting room but for the church as a whole). Let them team up with other adults so the service is intergenerational.

Some young people could also serve as an escort service to seat elderly or handicapped people. Others could make sure visitors get to their appropriate religious education classroom and introduce them to people already there who can help them feel welcomed and get them involved right away.

You can always pull the "unofficial" welcoming action of greeting people even though you don't have a welcoming committee name tag or aren't wearing a flower or passing out church bulletins. Just be friendly and welcome people to church. Welcome long time members as well as guests.

Many adults are intimidated by young people and wait for young people to take the initiative to make contact. They aren't necessarily unfriendly. They simply don't understand why teens dress the way they do, why they wear their hair in certain styles, or talk so strangely. They might not even recognize you since your appearance has changed so much in the past decade--while they pretty much look the same as they always have.

HABITAT
FOR
HUMANITY

 abitat for Humanity is a non-profit organization dedicated to eliminating homelessness by providing low-cost housing for individuals who cannot afford a home. The low cost of a home is made possible by donated labor. Former President Jimmy Carter is the honorary chairperson of Habitat for Humanity.

Volunteers are needed to help construct homes and perform other important duties such as fund raising and public relations. Whether or not you have experience, your time is valuable. Because Habitat for Humanity has no administrative expenses, all money goes to housing and volunteers are appreciated even more. Look in your local phone book for a chapter in your neighborhood. If a chapter is not listed, contact the international headquarters for the nearest chapter:

> Habitat for Humanity
> 121 Habitat Street
> Americus, GA 31709-3498
> (912) 924-6935

Volunteers work in the evenings or on weekends. This flexibility is great for individuals or groups who have busy schedules.

HOME AVAILABLE

The ministry of the Church is not limited to activities within the walls of the church building. In fact, some very significant ministries occur outside of those walls. Some people won't step foot inside a church, but they would come to your home. Is your home available?

Because some gatherings occur in large houses, such as a youth pool party at a wealthy business person's mansion, many are prone to deduce that their relatively small house could never be utilized for ministry. Not true!

The critical element is not space, but attitude. Are you able to be hospitable by welcoming others into your house? If you are, make your home available. You may need to pursue an actual event or gathering at your abode.

Your place may become an after-school hangout for kids who have nowhere to go. Perhaps it will serve as a spot for a small group Bible study or other support group. You don't have to have the entire house in immaculate condition to host guests. A living room or family room is all that is needed, and perhaps a nearby bathroom. You don't even have to serve refreshments.

Some people have a small house, but they have a full basement, large yard or access to a nearby park or other play area. Your house can be the gathering place for other activities. Have you offered it to groups in need of a place to gather? If not, start your own group!

HOTLINE VOLUNTEERS

There has been a real surge (and a really needed one, too) in emergency agencies that reach out to youth in times of crisis. Youth run away because of divorce, incest, drug abuse, confusion, pregnancy and more. Agencies that serve them are always in need of additional volunteer help. Some of the needs are:

- Phone counselors trained to deal with those contemplating suicide or having a rough time at home. Many times the agency will provide training for the counselor.
- Administrative volunteers - People who have interest in marketing, fund raising, accounting and more are needed to help agencies that are dependent on volunteers. (Experiences like this can improve your resume, too.)
- Advisory board - Young people are often needed on agency boards to help keep the organization relevant to youth culture. If asked to serve, say "YES!"

Here are some toll-free numbers for some nationally recognized youth services. Contact them for branch or affiliated organizations in your area.

Boys Town National Hotline 1-800-448-3000

Childhope (for homeless children) 1-804-359-4848

National Runaway Switchboard 1-800-621-4000

Covenant House Nineline 1-800-999-9999

HOUSE CLEANING SERVICE

Offer to have your group provide a once-a-week house cleaning service for people who could use a break. Offer the service for one month. A group of four or five can really clean up a home in less than an hour each week. Designate individuals who will dust, vacuum, wash dishes, do laundry, clean windows, mow lawns and take garbage to the dump. Be careful in the home. You never know which dish is 100 years old or which piece of clothing can't be machine washed.

Individuals who might need a house-cleaning break include:

- New Parents
- Recently hospitalized
- Recently moved or relocated
- Single parents
- Death in the family
- Recently divorced
- Older member
- Anyone who could use a break

HOUSE REPAIR SCAVENGER HUNT

Try this idea for an interesting twist on the scavenger hunt concept. First, locate a home that needs T.L.C. where an individual, because of physical or financial limitations, is not able to make the improvements themselves. Have a knowledgeable person (preferably the person who will lead your group when you make the repairs) list the materials that will be needed. Make sure you have measurements that are accurate.

Once you have the list, make enough copies for each team in your group. Then, in scavenger hunt fashion, select a neighborhood for each team and start knocking. Explain to the people what you are doing and ask if they would look at your list and see if they have some of the items. You'll be surprised at what people have - paint, windows, doors, carpet and wood! If they can help, be sure to carry a note pad to get their name, address and item they are donating. This information will prove useful if the donated item needs to be picked up later or if they need a letter/ receipt verifying their donation. Remember, while you can provide them with a receipt indicating their donation, the IRS requires the donor to establish the value.

IMMIGRANT MINISTRY

Immigrant families are often the most receptive to Christianity. With their major transition, many are in great need of assistance in adapting to their new culture. Here are five ways you can help immigrants make a smoother transition:

- English class - there are numerous, inexpensive textbooks you can use to teach English. You can even have them use a contemporary version of the Bible for their reading assignments.
- Organize free health clinics that offer routine check-ups and inoculations to immigrants who have no health coverage.
- Conduct a cultural understanding class that teaches the nuances of American culture and practice.
- Provide free or low cost child care for families.
- Hold information seminars on where things are in the community, such as locations of libraries, discount stores, schools, clinics and government agencies. (See "Welcome Wagon")

LANDSCAPING

Take your group on a tour of five or six possible locations that you can landscape or facelift. Once you have selected a site, contact the officials who are responsible for the area. Present them with your plans for the area and offer to do all the work on the site. You can provide the materials or if it's a big project, ask them to supply the items. Try to select a project that your group can complete in less than half a day. Morale tends to wane when projects are much longer.

Places you might check out:

- Parks
- Playground areas (offer to replenish sand in play areas)
- Historical Monuments
- Rest Areas
- Sidewalks
- Medians
- Tourist or Information Centers

55 LETTER OF AFFIRMATION

Just as notes of encouragement can brighten a person's day, a letter of affirmation can do the same. A letter is a more formal approach and can make a significant impact on public figures or other key leaders who are apt to receive more criticism and demands rather than affirmations and thank yous. Such people often keep a file of these refreshing written messages, reviewing them during moments of frustration or depression.

To be more meaningful, don't just write "You're a nice person." Give something specific you appreciate about the person, such as "taking a public stand last week against NIMBY (Not In My Back Yard--take care of the homeless away from my neighborhood) took a lot of courage. I'm with you 150 percent!"

If you don't know enough about the person to write about something specific, address a general need in a specific way. For example, "I know you face a lot of pressures because of the public nature of your job. I want you to know that I'm praying for your inner peace to be constant, especially when things are swirling about you." And then really do pray for the person!

The types of people to target for such a letter include government officials, pastors, educators, parents, contemporary Christian musicians, company presidents and CEOs. You can add your own likely candidates. It may become a regular activity for you. And others will be encouraged because of it.

56 LETTERS OR CARDS FOR BIRTHDAYS

ome churches keep a file with the birthdays of all their members. But that doesn't guarantee that those members receive a birthday card or letter from the church. Help your pastor give a yearly reminder of celebration and appreciation to the members by generating a birthday letter the pastor can sign and members will receive on (or close to) their birthday. One birthday letter can be put on a computer and can serve as the form for one year before a new one needs to be written.

Once a week have the computer print out the birthday letters for the members who will have a birthday in the next week. Put these on the pastor's desk for his/her signature. All they have to do is sign it, fold it, put it in the stamped and addressed envelope that accompanies the birthday letter, and drop it in the mail.

You can do a similar thing for your youth group, too. You may want to personalize it a little more by creating homemade birthday cards. These can still be mailed, or you can personally deliver them or do a door bell ring-and-run surprise stop. This could be part of your regular written affirmations (see "Letters of Affirmation").

LETTERS TO THE EDITOR

Exercise your right to speak out in response to what's happening. Put it in the form of a letter to the editor of a publication that has presented an issue or event that sparks your interest. This could be a local newspaper for local items, a church publication for religious interests, a magazine for whatever they've published.

Your letter might be in disagreement or in support of what has been printed already. Or it could be a combination of both. In addition to writing the letter yourself, you might also recruit others to join you.

When writing a letter to the editor, express your personal opinion and then state what it's based on. Spell out the implications that may be unstated. What would happen if everyone put this into practice?

If a group of individuals want to write letters to the editor, it might be worthwhile to first have a group discussion about the issue. This can help to clarify things for some of the writers and may spur others or deepen their conviction(s).

Sometimes a letter can be improved by having someone else read it and respond to their immediate impression of it. You might want to share it with someone who hasn't been involved in the "writing campaign" such as a family member, neighbor, friend or other church member. Are there parts that are unclear? Are you making quantum leaps in logic? Are you simply wrong?

After editing your letter, mail it to the editor. You've given your input. Who knows? Maybe it will be published in an upcoming issue and others will think more about it because of your action based on reflection.

A similar writing campaign can be directed to a government official, such as a city, state, or federal government representative. You should expect a letter of response from the office of your elected government official!

LITERATURE DISTRIBUTION

on't chuck this idea until you read the whole page. Yes, literature distribution has been given a bad name because some people have been too confrontational in handing out literature or becaues the materials available were not relevant.

Why not track down magazine display racks that are not used and fill them with literature that deals with family issues or relationship building. Material that does address more direct spiritual issues are also welcomed. However, be sure to avoid tracts that are filled with one cliché after another and really are written for a person who is already a Christian. Christian bookstores carry lots of good materials that are direct and yet fresh.

Then set up your display with the carefully chosen literature in the area of your choice. Check the rack every week or so for restocking.

MISSIONARY PEN PAL

Most missionaries have the spiritual gift of ministering to others in another culture. The blessings they receive by being used by God in these unique circumstances far outweigh the "comforts of home" they have foregone to be missionaries. Their lives are immersed into their mission and they rarely have free time to even give much thought to their homeland.

Even so, they usually appreciate hearing from home. Jot a one-page letter every once in awhile (perhaps monthly) to a missionary telling them what's going on in your life, in the country, and in their hometown (if you know). You can develop a relationship with one person, one family, or bounce around from one missionary to another.

To find out what missionaries you could contact, ask your local pastor (your congregation might be sponsoring a missionary) or the missions branch of your denomination. Christian colleges might also be able to put you in touch with mission agencies or share with you names of their students who currently are serving as student missionaries (SMs).

You can send photos, magazines, M & Ms, soft toilet paper (if they don't have these amenities). If they have a tape recorder send a taped message. Interview other people for the tape. Record a song from your church service. If they have a VCR, make and send a video!

If the missionary family has teens, you might be helping to prevent some of the "culture shock" they experience when they return home because you kept them up to date on what is happening in your world. Plus, your world will be enlarged by plugging into theirs. Who knows, your youth group may choose to do a short-term mission trip where your missionary pen pal serves, or your church may become a supporting "sister church" for their endeavors!

MOVING DAY ASSISTANCE

When people move into a community or move away from it, they probably could use a few extra hands at key moments in the process.

For those who are moving away (besides a farewell party) offer service certificates that can be redeemed during the packing process or on moving day. For example, two hours of free child-care in their house so they can have uninterrupted time to pack and still be available to their kid(s) if need be. Another would be one evening to help box up the kitchen cupboards, etc.

On moving day itself, the gift certificates could be redeemed for such services as:

* Loading boxes and furniture
* Final cleaning of the house once everything's out
* A picnic lunch brought over to feed the helpers
* Child care
* Pick up truck (if just a move across town or to take a load of trash to the dump)

Somebody could also document the event with a camera, tape recorder, or video camera.

For those moving into your area, similar services could be available, as well as quick tours of the town, free meals to people's houses (while the new family is still unpacking), gift certificates to join specific people for fun, social activities to integrate them with new friends, etc. (see "Welcome Wagon").

NEIGHBORHOOD BIBLE CLUB

perated in a way similar to VBS (see Vacation Bible School), a Neighborhood Bible Club isn't limited to one or two weeks a year. It runs the entire year or throughout the school year. It functions as a weekly VBS and can take place at the church or in a home.

Recruit local neighborhood children for a time of singing, Bible stories, games, and other activities. Good times to schedule are a weekday right after school or right after supper. Perhaps the best time for your area would be Tuesday afternoons from 3:00-5:00. Maybe the ideal time would be Wednesday evenings from 6:30-8:00. Remember that you need a time that works for the children and the volunteers to staff the program.

Another way this differs from VBS is that it requires a long-term commitment on the part of the leaders as well as reminders to the children that "Today is Tuesday--which means Neighborhood Bible Club right after school!" The leaders aren't taxed as heavily since there is a one-week break between sessions.

Curriculum guides for the Neighborhood Bible Club would be similar to what you'd utilize for VBS. It might be easier to recruit some one-time volunteers for a week or month of NBC than to recruit them for VBS. Some might choose to be part of both. Ideally the children will become integrated into your religious education program and the rest of the life of your church.

NOTES OF ENCOURAGEMENT

 o you have the gift of encouragement? Jot a quick note to people and get it to them. You can use something as simple as a post-it note. Or you could be more elaborate and use Hallmark or homemade cards.

Here are a few tips:

- Make it short and simple - "You really made me feel included in the group yesterday--thanks!"
- Write something specific - "All the supplies were right where we needed them for VBS, including the glue bottles (all full)--you're incredible!"
- Focus on something current - "I went back to clean up after our snacks last night and--surprise-you'd done it all. Thanks for being so helpful!"
- Personalize it - "Just when I felt like I was the only one helping out, I found out you had been working on it all along and had recruited three other people to help us. I sure have a lot to learn. Thanks for being such a positive example for me."

Sometimes it's fun to do the notes anonymously. In such cases, give enough information so the recipient knows what you're writing about, or else make it a general note of encouragement (which protects your anonymity more easily), such as "God's doing great things through you--keep it up!" or "God thinks you're awesome, and the rest of us think so, too." You can also share a verse of scripture, such as "You are the light of the world--shine on!"

Notes can be slipped into people's lockers, into their school books, or even into their sock drawer at home, although it might require some help from friends sworn to silence.

OFFICE FLOWER BLITZ

ontact a couple of florists in your community and ask them to keep you informed when they have too many flowers because of a canceled order or an over purchase. In such situations you can buy carnations for less than 50 cents each.

Select an office building as your target. You can choose one that has three employees or 50 - it's up to you! Purchase the flowers and attach a small hand-written note with words of encouragement. Contact the boss or manager of the office and arrange for a time of delivery. Then have your group personally present every employee with a flower and note. Remember, you are on the boss's time. You can chat with the employees for a couple of minutes but be ready to move on.

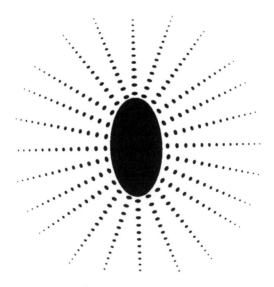

ORGAN DRIVE

Even in our medically advanced society, body organs are still needed desperately. People die every day because of the shortage of vital organs. Organizations that encourage individuals to donate their organs exist in almost every community.

To sponsor a local organ drive, contact your local organ donor agency or contact the national headquarters at 804-330-8500. Then obtain a mall management's permission to set up a table near a main entrance where you can encourage people to sign-up as an organ donor on their driver's license, picture I.D. or organ donor card.

Frequently organ donor organizations will supply you with organ donor stickers for a driver's license or an organ donor I.D. card that can be placed in a person's wallet. Even if your state offers the option of becoming a donor when obtaining your driver's license, remember that many people don't take the time to sign up for this important program.

Stickers can always be placed on a person's license at anytime. Organ donor agencies should be able to provide you with those stickers. They say that being an organ donor is giving the gift that keeps on giving.

65 OUTREACH WITH OTHER AREA CHURCHES

The days of highly competitive interchurch rivalries are gone in most areas, although some still might be battling it out to see who's the biggest or the best, or feeling they are the only true church and all others are a farce. Most Christians are open simply to reaching others for Jesus, especially those who aren't even Christians.

There might be a ministerial fellowship of area pastors or even area youth pastors in your community. Join forces for an outreach event that targets non-Christians. It could be a small-scaled event that involves only the local people or it could be as big as sponsoring a Carman concert, complete with arena and lots of counselors on hand for those who accept Christ.

One of the major keys is to get representative input from the area churches. These are the people who will get others involved. Otherwise only one or two churches may carry an unfair portion of the weight. For youth evangelism, coordinating with Youth for Christ or Campus Crusade or some other parachurch organization provides a more natural central planning structure.

The outreach event itself must be agreed upon by the sponsoring organizations. Keep in mind that to reach unchurched young people you need to go to them rather than expecting them to come knocking on your church door! This should influence both what the event is and the venue (where it is held). The actual event might be a concert, picnic, sports day, or amusement park or water slide park with a sand pit volleyball tournament and religious concert and youth speaker in the evening.

To pull this off takes a lot of preparation and follow up. But the benefits for those who join God's people, as well as for those already in the church, are out of this world!

PARENT-TEEN SEMINAR

ith the onset of adolescence many young people and most of their parents enter a strange, challenging, troublesome period of adjustment. Parents want their children to be responsible and adolescents want freedom from their parents. The transition can be quite traumatic. One of the keys is to maintain or increase communication and have an openness to adjustments in the relationship.

Most Christian bookstores carry parenting materials that could easily be made into a seminar, if they aren't already in that format. Or you can create your own. One key is to have some presentations by the adolescents and some by the parents. A facilitator can help both groups articulate their interests and concerns, plus make sure the parents listen rather than deny, dominate or scold.

One method to open up the issues is to have parents and adolescents separated to discuss a topic, such as the needs of adolescents and the needs of parents. Lead them in their separate discussions and help them come to conclusions. They can even spend time discussing what they think the other group would come up with. Then bring them together to share their results.

Another method is to have anonymous questions written out by the participants. Form "temporary families" by mixing the participants so that parents and adolescents are with someone other than their own family members. Present one question at a time and have the participants answer it in their "temporary family" groups.

Other methods include panel discussions, role plays, hypothetical situations families must deal with, and commitment or covenant services.

PARKING METER MAYHEM

Parking meter mayhem is a fun and simple activity for almost anyone. Stake out an area that has metered parking. Good areas to scout are libraries, post offices, city or county buildings and shopping areas, especially in a downtown area.

Two people will be needed to cover each side of a square block for a total of eight for each block. As cars pull into parking spots, volunteers place coins in the meter for the unsuspecting driver. This simple act creates a tremendous amount of goodwill. Say "hello" and then back away. You don't want the driver to think you're about to steal their car or assault them.

If you wish, you could hand out pencils, stickers or small cards that say, "Jesus loves you" or "Your meter has been covered, compliments of the King" - and we're not talking Elvis here, either!

Note: Depending on the location, parking meters can run from five cents for 15 minutes up to 25 cents for 10 minutes. Have each participant bring as many coins as possible. You may also want to supplement each person's stash.

PEER COUNSELING

lmost all humans receive counseling, even if it's not from certified or officially trained counselors or therapists. We most frequently turn to friends for counseling, although we may not call it that.

What's basically involved is learning how to implement listening skills--quite an art! A group of peer counselors meets regularly (perhaps once a week) to learn and practice specific skills. They then get lots of opportunities to practice their new skills in the real life situations outside of the instructional sessions.

This was never intended to be a replacement for deep or intense therapy. The reality is that many people who need a counselor never go to a trained counselor, and most of us do informal counseling. So why not at least learn how to listen a little better?

Complete training curriculum is available in these resources:

Peer Counseling in Youth Groups
Barbara Varenhorst
San Francisco, CA: Harper & Row, 1983
ISBN 0-06-250890-3

Real Friends: Becoming the Friend You'd Like to Have
Barbara Varenhorst
San Francisco, CA: Harper & Row, 1983
ISBN 0-06-250890-3

Training Teenagers for Peer Ministry
Barbara Varenhorst with Lee Sparks
Loveland, CO: Group, 1988
ISBN 0931-529-23-9

PERSON OF THE YEAR BANQUET

ne way to affirm the positive things in your community is to honor those who are responsible. Examine your local papers to discover the individuals who seem to be active in a number of ways. You can also call your local paper, Chamber of Commerce, Rotary club, Lions club, etc., for recommendations of names. Once you have your list down to the three top candidates, vote among your group to determine the winner.

Then plan a "Person of the Year" banquet and honor this active citizen of your community. You can even have a nice plaque made up for them.

Ask them in advance to make a short speech on the subject of community service. You can even ask the mayor of your town to present the plaque to the recipient. Contact your local paper, radio and TV stations for possible coverage.

70

PLAN A PARTY

o much of our time is spent in planning social activities for our own churches. Yet we have little social contact with thousands of churches.

One way to remedy the situation is to throw a party for another church's youth group. Contact the youth leader or youth pastor at a church similar in size to your church. Select a date that works for both groups. Then meet with the youth leader or youth pastor. Visit the room the leader recommends for the party to get a feel for the place. Take along the youth who will help you decorate the room and arrange the refreshments.

The party can either be announced with a personal invitation by your group or it can be a surprise. Whichever choice you make, the party hinges on well-planned mixers and icebreakers that get your group mixed with theirs. If you don't do it early in the party, the two groups will never mix.

Keep the party short, maybe an hour or so. Even with effective mixers, an hour will "stretch" them socially. By then many are ready to return to the "safety" of their respective groups. Those who want to keep mixing certainly will!

POWDER-PUFF CAR REPAIR COURSE

Offer a ten-week course on car maintenance and repair to the young women in your community. Each week can feature a different aspect of car repair and maintenance. Topics that could be covered include flat tire repair, oil change, tune-ups, fluids check (oil, transmission, brake, windshield wiper, etc.), long-trip inspections, what to watch out for when buying a vehicle, and what to do in case of an accident.

Advertise your course through public service time on TV, radio, and newspaper ads. When selecting the instructor, be sure to choose someone who is a good teacher and can explain instructions simply. To provide the best instruction you may want to have a car for every four to six people with assistants located at each car.

Note: An increasing number of guys don't have a clue when it comes to even simple tasks in car repair. A course could be well received by them, too. Remember that society expects guys to know about cars. You may not want to have guys and girls take the course together - the guys' egos may not be able to take it!

72 PUBLIC SERVANT APPRECIATION DAY

Select a public servant your group wishes to thank for their contributions to the community. Some examples might include:

- ◆ Police Department
- ◆ Fire Department
- ◆ City or County Hall
- ◆ District Attorney's office
- ◆ Paramedics or 9-1-1 operators
- ◆ Chamber of Commerce
- ◆ United Way office
- ◆ Community Shelters
- ◆ National Guard
- ◆ Library
- ◆ Maintenance Shop for City, County or State
- ◆ School Janitors
- ◆ Secretaries

Contact the chief or director of the place you wish to visit and arrange for the best time for your group to arrive. Try to arrive during a shift change to include the most people. Take cookies and a drink along with a "Thank You" banner signed by your group, church or school expressing appreciation for making your communities a better or safer place to live.

RADIO OR TV TALK SHOW

Contact your local TV or radio station (Christian or non-Christian) about broadcasting a show that addresses young people's issues.

Your group can be involved in different aspects of the program production. For example, one team could review new music or share reviews that help listeners or viewers make good choices. Another team can address issues such as suicide, substance abuse, abortion, sex, you name it. Another team can be watching for people in the community who are making a difference in a positive way through education and/or modeling.

Even though there may be production costs, sponsors may not be too hard to find if your program is relevant and upbeat.

WE ARE

HIS

HANDS

RAINY DAY CURBSIDE SERVICE

ot everyone carries an umbrella when it rains, but most people get wet when walking in the rain. Some who go to church choose to "make a mad dash for it" from their car to the building, even if they have to park 100 yards away. Maybe they're praying for a lull in the rain just as they arrive!

Get a group of young people to provide umbrella coverage for these mad-dashers. Some people will be dropped off near the protective coverings of the church and may need an umbrella only for a few steps. Others will need the full coverage from where they park their car until they get inside the church.

Try to collect large umbrellas rather than compact ones. It would also be a good idea to have the young people wear overcoats or raincoats and possibly galoshes, especially since they are apt to be making several trips.

Another option is to have a valet service, which works very nicely if there's one covered driveway for people to be dropped off at church. Of course, the valet drivers would need to be careful and trust-inspiring in how they handle the cars!

RAKE & RUN
(OR SNOW SHOVEL & RUN)

ere's a seasonal activity that can be done as a group, plus you can mix in a little bit of intrigue. Travel as a group in a van or some pickups and stop at places that are in obvious need of raking/leaf removal (or snow removal). The group bounds out of their vehicles and quickly does their work, hopefully before the people inside can say "boo!"

One catch is that some people, including some elderly people, use leaf raking or snow shoveling as a form of exercise. Such people rarely appreciate of your work if it results in stopping their exercise program. And having them join you for a house or two may be too quick-paced for what they had in mind.

You can prevent this misdirection of service by ringing the doorbell with the whole group poised ready for the "go" sign. If people get in a tizzy because you've removed the leaves they wanted to rake, simply distribute them back over the lawn and leave--or bring back a shipment from the next yard you service!

Remember to treat other people's property with respect. Bring your own rake or shovel. Dress appropriately--layers are a good idea to keep warm between forays and to peel off as you work up a sweat. Conclude at a pre-arranged place for some refreshments, such as hot cider and cookies.

RECYCLING PROGRAM

ne obvious way to "save the planet" is to recycle. Some counties provide recycling containers at public places such as shopping center parking lots. Others have curbside service with separate containers for newspapers, plastics, glass bottles and cans.

Recycling center locations can be found in the yellow pages of your phone directory. Most recycling centers will take the following:

- ◆ Aluminum cans
- ◆ Glass (bottles, jars or other containers)
- ◆ Plastic (jugs, bottles or other containers)
- ◆ Paper (white, colored, computer, newspaper and cardboard)
- ◆ Anything else the recycling center takes

Seasonal recycling can take place by recycling Christmas trees or telephone books. You may need to advertise your recycling and perhaps go through some neighborhoods at monthly intervals to pick up goods to recycle. This requires planning, commitment and follow through in addition to adequate advertising and informing.

This can even be a fund raiser for your youth group, or you can take the proceeds from your collection and apply it to other environment concerns, such as planting a tree or planting wildflower seeds by a barren roadside.

REST AREAS

Hang-out at rest areas with donuts and drinks to hand out to people as they come and go. If you want to make the biggest impact on the most people, set your group up at a rest area during a long weekend. Be sure to get permission from your state highway system office.

Take an atlas with you just in case someone is lost or looking for a better way to get where they are going. If you live in an area that has things to do that would interest visitors, make a list of them with their address and a little map, when they are open and what they cost. This information could be very useful to tourists.

Brainstorm among your group for game ideas they play when they travel. Some examples would include making a list of all states you see on car license plates or having a contest to see who can make it through the alphabet first by spotting each letter, in order, as seen on license plates, road and commercial signs. Once you have four or five game ideas, type them up on a sheet of paper and make several copies to hand out to travelers.

RUNS OR DRIVES FOR THE NEEDY

lmost every home has items no longer used but could be of great value to a needy person. Contact a local homeless or runaway shelter to determine their needs. Coats, blankets, sleeping bags, underwear, children's clothing, toys and food are among the many items that helping agencies need.

Compile a list of needed items; then create a flier that itemizes them, along with the agency that will receive the donated goods. Determine the number of fliers you will have made up (there are about 30 homes per square block when you count all four sides) and distribute them one week before you plan to pick up the items.

In the flier, mention that donated items should be placed on front porches on the specified pick-up day. Arrange for a truck on pick-up day and drive it down the street where you passed out the fliers. Group members can go down both sides of the street collecting items. A ten-block area can be covered by an average sizeed group in 30 to 40 minutes.

Note: If donors desire a receipt, you can provide them with one that lists their donated items. The IRS will not allow you to determine the value of the donation. The responsibility of valuation rests with the donor, not you. All you can do is verify that your non-profit organization received the items as a donation.

SENIOR CITIZEN ERRANDS

The stereotypical picture of a senior citizen spending the entire day sitting in a rocking chair certainly isn't true of lots of senior citizens. In fact, most would like to do even more than they are currently doing, but they need a little help in doing it since their physical abilities aren't quite what they used to be.

Team up with a senior citizen (see "Adopt-a-Grandparent") or a home for senior citizens and be the extra help that is needed to keep them active and alive. Some may want to purchase a little gift for a grandchild, but they don't feel safe driving since their reflexes aren't as quick Those teenagers on the road drive so fast and have no patience! If you drive them to a store, they'll be able to buy that gift. They also might ask for your input on what the gift should be. Others may want to get a few personal items or groceries.

There might be just one or two errands they need help with, such as going to the post office to buy stamps or getting some film developed. Some might be losing their ability to write letters. Would you write one for them as they dictate it to you? Some might want to make a cassette tape, but don't know how to work these newfangled things. Do you know how to record on a cassette tape?

Doing errands for senior citizens doesn't mean doing everything for them so they can sit in their rocking chair longer. It means joining them in a variety of activities so they aren't stuck in their rocking chair. Instead they are able to do more activities once again because someone is helping them do things they can no longer do on their own.

SHORT-TERM MISSION TRIPS

ere's an intense service activity that might initiate some people into a service lifestyle. Frequently these are cross-cultural experiences in which young people serve others through construction of urgently needed buildings, repair work, evangelism, or even ecological concerns.

Typically the more unusual it is (building a church in the Amazon jungle), the higher the interest and the higher the cost compared to a local service project (cleaning the storage rooms at the church).

If you choose to do a short-term mission trip, try to involve as many people as possible, even though only a handful may actually go on the trip. Others can be prayer partners, assist in fund raising, collect supplies, help in the send off and return experiences, assist in debriefing the experience, support with encouragement and hearing the stories.

You can go it alone or team up with agencies who have been over the trail before. Such agencies include:

1. Maranatha Volunteers International (916-920-1900) focuses on the construction of churches, schools, hospitals/clinics, orphanages, and other urgently needed buildings throughout the world, although especially in Central America.
2. Group Workcamps (800-747-6060) provides construction and repairs for low-income families, primarily in different parts of the U.S. during the summer.
3. Adventures in Missions (407-790-0394) Construction projects and evangelism primarily in Central American countries.

One excellent resource is the *Maranatha Guide to Adventure* by Steve and Debbie Case. A 3-component resource that includes a manual for leaders, a video for participants and a card deck of discussion starter questions. To order, call (916) 920-1900.

SHORT-TERM MISSION TRIP WELCOME HOME PARTY

Have a welcome home party for your short-term mission trip participants upon their arrival home or shortly thereafter if they are likely to be too exhausted immediately upon their return. An unearthly hour, such as their arrival at 1:00 AM might actually add zest to the event!

They're likely to have culture shock on their return. Be aware that they might come back as crusaders--admonishing you to sell all you have and send the money to the *truly* needy people in the world. They might also be a little reactionary if you try to show too much understanding since *they* are the ones who went through their recent experiences--you didn't!

Plan to have some of their favorite foods. Give them time to share some of their experiences. Do it both in small groups and in a large group so everyone has a chance to share, and yet there are larger group information and sharing times, too. There can be happy times of reunion, serious moments of reflection, integration, and time to laugh and get caught up.

This is a golden opportunity to have the returnees sign up for other service projects that might not be as glamorous but certainly worthwhile as they continue a lifestyle of service. You might also start a fund raising drive for a specific project the group identifies for the people they just left.

Invite the short-term mission supporters. Briefly share with the returnees what has been going on while they were away (after they've given their report of their trip). This could be done as a news report or skit style. Identify a time for more sharing and integration once pictures have been developed, video footage has been edited, and the rest of the church family can participate (such as during the worship service next weekend).

SMOKING CESSATION PROGRAM

While it's out of vogue to smoke in many parts of North America these days, millions of people still do it. And many would like to stop (and stay stopped!). Some people pay lots of money to attend seminars or join support groups to be freed of the tobacco habit.

One successful program that comes as a complete package for groups and can be conducted with relative ease is called "Breathe Free." It's based on the concept that the withdrawals from nicotine can be stopped in just three days, provided you completely stop your smoking and the inside of your body is flushed out with lots of fluids. The cost for the director's kit for "Breathe Free" is $59 and can be purchased by calling 800-548-8700.

To enhance self-control, a buddy system is set up to get through the periodic strong cravings. After that, it's simply a matter of getting over the psychological addiction. Thousands have been freed of their smoking habit for good by going through this program.

Special attention is given to motivation, although the program assumes that the participant wants to stop smoking in the first place. To add a little challenge to the motivational aspects, try offering the program to high school students nearby. In fact, some high schools will require that their students caught smoking must attend a smoking cessation program. You can offer that program, although the students might participate primarily to get out of trouble rather than because they really want to stop smoking. What a challenge!

SOCIAL INJUSTICE

o you know someone who has been treated unjustly? Has it turned out to be something that could not be settled between the two of them? Is one of them bullied by the other? Has a landlord or government agency or big business taken advantage of someone who doesn't know how to put up a defense when mistreated?

There are a number of things a local group of citizens can do, such as:

- ◆ Set up a volunteer council of professionals who agree to meet as needs arise to provide legal or financial advice to the poor. Attorneys, accountants, business people and counselors can be great candidates for such a council.
- ◆ Start a letter writing campaign to elected officials to involve them in helping to straighten things out or correct injustices.
- ◆ Invite a representative from Amnesty International or the Association of Public Justice to come speak to your group.
- ◆ Have a pastor preach a sermon on how Christians should relate to social injustice.

There are many other meaningful activities that can help victims of social injustice. For more information, contact one of the following organizations:

Amnesty International
322 Eighth Ave.
New York, NY 10001
1-800-AMNESTY

Association for Public Justice
321 8th Street
Washington, DC 20002

SPONSOR A CHILD

Instead of being overwhelmed by the fact that 40,000 children starve to death each day, make a difference by sponsoring a child. Several agencies provide food and medicine for a child and they will send you a photo and some background information about the child. Some agencies include religious instruction as well. You might be able to choose the gender and what part of the world "your" child is from, such as Africa, Asia or Latin America.

Sponsoring a child requires a long-term commitment since monthly payments are necessary. It can be glamorous for awhile, but soon it becomes a test to see if your commitment to service is a lifestyle or just a flash in the pan.

Here are some agencies that can help you feed starving children:

- Children International
  P. O. Box 419413
  Kansas City, MO 64179-0613
  $10/month

- Food for the Hungry
  P. O. Box E
  Scottsdale, AZ 85252
  $22/month

- Sponsor a Child
  Reach International
  PO Box 34
  Berrien Springs, MI 49103
  1-800-869-1412
  $15/month

- World Vision
  Childcare Sponsorship
  Pasadena, CA 91191-0119
  $20/month

- Compassion International
  PO Box 7000
  Colorado Springs, CO 80933-9849
  $24/month

SPONSORING CONTESTS

With a little creativity for prizes, a number of contests could be held to draw attention to specific issues.

For example, have a poster contest in which all churches are challenged to create posters that help draw attention to the issues of child abuse, hunger, homelessness, or the environment. Display the posters at a frequented store.

Another activity could be a song writing contest that addresses a community issue, and the winners get to sing their song on the radio. Speaking contests are another effective way to address an issue in your community.

Choose your issues carefully. Make sure the issues represent community felt needs so it's not just your hobbyhorse.

WE ARE

HIS

HANDS

SPORTS CLINICS

If eight to ten weeks is too much of a commitment for your group (see "Coaching"), try a week-long sports camp or clinic. Choose whichever sport you and your group feel most comfortable with. Pick your time carefully. If you hold a football or basketball camp during the summer, you might find local college players willing to stop in for a brief visit. Their celebrity appearance will add to the excitement of the event.

You can offer your clinic as a one-day event or start it on a Monday night and go through Thursday evening. Plan on a couple of hours each night. Structure your time carefully, scheduling approximately 60 percent of your time working on skills and technique and 40 percent in scrimmage.

If you have expenses, charge a small fee of $5 or $10 for each participant. Be sure you publicize the event well. Places to post announcements are in local public schools, grocery store bulletin boards, the local YMCA/YWCA and community parks. Inform any coaches of school teams about your plans. Not only will they help promote the event, they may offer to assist you.

SPORTS EQUIPMENT DRIVE

ost cities and towns have fairly active sports programs for young people. With budget cutbacks hitting recreational programs hard, your group might consider contacting the recreational director of the city or county program, YMCA/YWCA, or the Boys and Girls Club director to learn of their equipment needs.

Create a list of the needed items and submit them along with an article of explanation to your local paper, radio and TV stations and let the drive begin! Your group will most likely find support from the Lions Club, Rotary, Kiwanis and Chamber of Commerce if you contact them far enough in advance. (Remember, they have their fund raising projects, too.)

In some instances, sporting goods manufacturers might respond favorably to letters requesting equipment. Also, contact any professional sports teams in your community and request their involvement.

SUMMER CAMP SPONSOR-A-KID

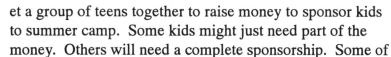

Get a group of teens together to raise money to sponsor kids to summer camp. Some kids might just need part of the money. Others will need a complete sponsorship. Some of the kids might help you in the fund raising. Summer camp can be a fun time and a life-changing experience for children. Some kids mark their week at summer camp as the start of their spiritual awakening or commitment, especially if it was a church-sponsored camp.

Selecting who receives the sponsorship will put your young people into the unique position of playing the role of God in determining who gets the goods. It's an awesome and frequently frustrating position to be in! Who is worthy? Who is needy? What right do you have to determine this?

Here are a few ideas for raising the funds:

- **Change Collection** - Solicit friends to put their pocket change into a common purse each day before they leave school or some other opportune time.
- **Brown Bagging It** - Donate the money from 1 meal a week they would usually purchase. This might mean getting up a little earlier on that day to make a brown bag lunch.
- **Match Me** - Ask adults or business owners or parents to match your funds so they double or triple as you put in money. You may need to put a cap on the amount for people to make a commitment for matching funds (up to $50, etc.).
- **Junk Food Fast** - At the times you would usually purchase some junk food, save the money for the summer camp fund. Do this for two or four weeks. Then have a pig-out party!
- **Car Wash** - Do it for free and ask car owners to donate as much as they would like to your cause--sponsoring kids to summer camp.

TAPES OF
WORSHIP SERVICE

ome churches already record their worship services. If yours doesn't, it doesn't need to be a complicated process. If a sound system is used, all you have to do is plug a tape deck into the sound system and record what goes through the system. You should get written permission from the speaker to record and duplicate the sermon.

Duplicating the tapes can be done on a relatively inexpensive dual cassette tape deck or wiring one tape deck to another. High speed duplicators are much more efficient, but much more costly. You might want to propose to your church board that they invest in such a machine so your worship services can be shared more easily with others. Blank tapes, especially in bulk quantities, don't cost much.

Deliver tapes of the worship service to those who would like to have been present, but weren't for various reasons. This could include shut-ins, members who were out of town. relatives of the presenter(s), or potential members who might be interested in your church services.

Providing the same service with video tape might be a quantum step for some, but easily within range for others. The costs are likely to escalate more quickly, especially if the quality matters. But it may be well worth the investment.

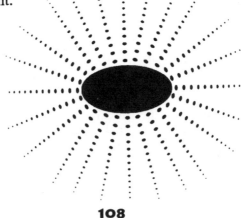

TOY COLLECTION AND DISTRIBUTION

During the Christmas season some groups become involved in a highly organized toy collection drive. You can invite lots of people to participate through donations or actually purchasing toys and dropping them off at assigned locations.

The other basic detail is who will receive the gifts. You might be in contact with an agency that can connect you with needy children. Some prefer to deliver the toys quietly to the parent(s) and let them give them to the child(ren) rather than being the joy givers at the parent's expense.

One youth group simply collected stuffed animals, including some that weren't brand new. They dressed one person up as Santa and headed to an apartment complex they knew was a low income area. When some older teens roaming the complex asked them what they were up to, the members of the youth group told them. The older teens then escorted them to the apartments where there would be small children who would want to see Santa and receive stuffed animals.

TRANSPORTATION SERVICE

Nowadays churches frequently serve a much larger area than their immediate neighborhood. In fact, some people will drive 30-60 minutes just to get to a particular church of their choice or for a special program.

Some people who would like to attend are prevented from doing so because they lack transportation. Public transportation might not serve either their area or the church area very well.

People who are apt to need transportation services are those without vehicles, such as low income people, convalescent or retirement home residents, young people without a driver's license, etc. Sometimes a combination of a personal invitation and transportation service is all people need to become involved.

The actual transportation might be in personal vehicles, church vans, or even church buses. Young people frequently are happy to drive around. Make sure they are safety conscious and have adequate directions. It might be inconvenient for the young people--such as an early morning pick up for church when the youth would rather be sleeping in.

It's also a good idea to keep in mind the type of vehicle the person would like to ride in. A person driving a Porsche might assume that anyone would like to ride in his/her car, but a group from a retirement center would probably prefer riding together in a van. Besides, those Porsches are so low to the ground, it's hard to get in and out of them! A passenger van is much easier! Most young people would choose the Porsche over a van any day! Sometimes you have no choice, and some transportation beats no transportation--for most people.

TWELVE-STEP PROGRAM

We might be addicted to addiction programs. The 12-step program of Alcoholics Anonymous has spread to many other addictions to provide support groups and help for drugs, families affected by drug or alcohol use/abuse, eating disorders, grief/loss, sexual perversion and more. You can expect that people in your church, including some of the young people, are in need of these services, as well as those who aren't part of your church.

You may choose to host a 12-step program that has the leadership but is in need of a place to meet (usually once a week). Another possibility is to lead the group, provided you have competent and willing leaders. You could also join the 12-step group as a support person, even if you don't share in the specific addiction primarily dealt with in that group.

Plenty of resource materials abound in this area, including books and pamphlets. Check with existing community health service organizations to see how you can best fit in with the services and needs of your particular community.

93 VACATION BIBLE SCHOOL

Elementary school children need lots of activity, especially during their vacation times. Parents of these children frequently are in need of child care services. You can meet both of these needs, plus provide religious instruction for children and an opportunity for your young people to discover and implement their various spiritual gifts by means of a Vacation Bible School (VBS).

While a VBS can be elaborate, keep in mind these basic components of the program:

- **Religious Instruction** - can be in large groups (general session) or in small groups (age categories or break-out groups if your age category still has lots of people). Be flexible on the content by being sensitive to how much religious instruction the participants have had previously--some may be unfamiliar with basic Bible stories. Your methods should strive for involvement, activity, and intriguing stories rather than simply lecturing to the participants.
- **Arts and Crafts** - an activity that certainly demands involvement. Craft books and craft stores have age-appropriate items. Here's something tangible for the children to take with them each day.
- **Recreation** - an opportunity to expend some energy, plus a golden opportunity to practice social skills through games. Look for non-competitive types of games; be inclusive rather than exclusive.
- **Snacks** - a good follow up to recreation. Strike a balance between junk food and tofu carob raisin sawdust.

Complete VBS curriculum is available from:
Adventist Book Center 1-800-765-6955
David C. Cook Publishing 1-800-323-7543
Group Publishing 1-800-747-6060

VACATION WITH A PURPOSE

o you want to see the Grand Canyon? Washington D.C.?
Disney World? How about taking some company?
Sponsor a group tour (it can be small or large) to historic sites
of interest and offer to take your neighborhood kids. Your trip can be a
couple of days or a week - it's up to you. Some things to consider are:

- Ask other parents to come along. Carefully select the ones you work with - a vacation can turn into a dreaded trip if you choose the wrong person.
- Offer to, and complete an FBI background check on yourself and other chaperons. This service will help many parents feel more at ease.
- Consider your age limits carefully. Ten and above is a good span. Ten-year olds are more self-sufficient and have had enough school that they generally respond to parental-type guidance more easily.
- Contact schools or churches at strategic points on your route to arrange housing. They will usually let you sleep on the gym mats and use their shower facilities. Many times the kitchen facilities will also be made available for food preparation. This housing will reduce trip costs dramatically.
- Charge an adequate fee to cover food, transportation, ticket purchases or entrance fees.
- Be sure to obtain permission slips and medical release forms for each person in your group.

VIDEO CONTEST

Contact your local youth pastor and/or leaders in area churches and challenge them to video their group participating in some kind of service project. The edited tape is then set to a contemporary Christian song. Presto. You have a music video.

Choose a night when all the groups are invited to attend a youth rally featuring each of the music videos. An objective panel of judges can rate each video according to its content and contribution to the area of service. Not only does each group get involved in one service project, but they are also exposed to the service ideas of other groups. The progressive medium of a music video inspires them to try these ideas.

Get a video projector (even if you have to rent it, it's worth it) and the largest possible screen you can find. Also run your sound through a separate sound system - a video projector's weakness is that it can't match the large picture with good sound.

For a more detailed manual on this event, call Youth and Young Adult Ministries Consultants at 1-800-440-1670 and ask for the Mission Safari Manual. Cost: $39.

VISITATION PROGRAM FOR MISSING YOUTH

enerally speaking, when parents stop attending church so do their youth. It is also true that as parents empower their children to make decisions, some youth choose not to attend church. Knowing why a person has stopped attending is very important. However, getting them to come back should not be your main goal. Church member reclaiming experts say that your main goal should be the re-establishing of meaningful relationships.

Your pastor may know of an upcoming training event that will enable you to be more effective in your outreach. Steps to follow include:

- Obtain proper training
- Have a brain-storming session to come up with all the names you can.
- Do as much research as you can (without being snoopy) to determine why a youth stopped attending. It is very possible that the youth has stopped attending because of a strained relationship with another young person in your group. Spend a few sessions talking with your group about ways relationships in your group can be improved. Why invite someone back to a group that still has the same problems that encouraged them to leave?
- Divide among your group members the names of missing youth. If someone knows the missing youth already and feels comfortable visiting them, by all means, encourage them. However, don't force them. Sometimes a young person may feel too close to the situation to get more involved. Honor this request, too.
- Don't give up. Strive to have the best relationships possible.

WELCOME WAGON

When people are new to a community there are lots of basic items of information and services they need to discover. You can gather a packet of this information and give it to them.

People will need to know about utilities, such as electricity, gas, water, sewage, garbage pickup, etc., especially if their realtor or landlord hasn't informed them. They will also need information about the following services: banks nearby (and what services they have), grocery stores, laundromats and dry cleaners, barbers and beauticians, hardware stores and home repair stores, discount warehouses, shopping malls, churches, schools and day care centers, medical services (hospital, clinics, offices for physicians and dentists), parks, recreational facilities and leagues. Some merchants will be willing to offer discounts or other coupons to go into a welcome wagon kit.

Those are the obvious needs. What is just as necessary is developing new friendships. What individuals and families can you link up with the newcomers? What activities are ideal for getting acquainted? Do you have a congregation that is friendly or merely tolerant towards newcomers?

You can anticipate that for young people, many families move to new communities in sync with a school year (early or late summer). Are you ready to give special attention to these potential busy times? You might want to have a few people monitor things throughout the year, with extra helpers during "peak" seasons.

YARD SALE

 ontact all the families in your church to bring unwanted but salable items to the yard sale location the night before the sale. Don't wait for the day of the sale to have items dropped off - you'll have buyers there at least an hour before you open, making it almost impossible to receive new items.

Location is everything in a yard sale. If you live off of a busy road, display directional signs in a prominent area to maximize your visibility. Also run an ad in your paper informing people of the date, time and location. You might even mention a few of your nicer items.

Proceeds can be donated to a local runaway shelter or inner city youth program.

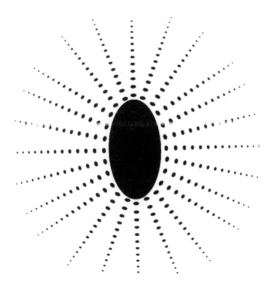

99

YOUTH AUCTION

ome Spring or Fall, many older members have yard work or odd jobs they are unable to do themselves. Why not help them and add some money to your youth budget?

Invite people to an event where they can bid on individual youth to "buy" them for one day or for a specific project. Have each youth walk forward and stand in the center of the room. People are encouraged to bid on each youth.

This activity is also an effective intergenerational event because it matches youth with older members--an association they rarely experience. You might consider offering punch and cookies afterwards to allow for some relationship building. All proceeds go for a designated cause such as a mission trip, orphanage or fund to help families in financial emergencies.

YOUTH GROUP SERVICE EXCHANGE

For those who have been around, it is understood that people living in poverty can be found in rural as well as urban settings.

If you live in an urban area, write to a church in a rural setting and invite them to spend a week during the summer doing service projects in your neighborhood. Then, next summer, return the favor. Have your group visit the rural neighborhood and spend a week in service projects there.

You might even want to plan some kind of retreat weekend where both groups get together in between summers to keep relationships alive. Such a program could lead to a sister church relationship.

YOUTH GROUP WORKCAMPS

Workcamps are an amazingly simple concept: Several youth groups band together to renovate housing for people who can't do the work themselves. Yet no other experience can so powerfully show your kids how to take what they know about God ... and live it.

At a workcamp, your kids will follow Christ's example. They'll explore what it really means to be a Christian, learning not only with their heads but also with their hands ... and their hearts. Teenagers at workcamps reach out by performing desperately needed home repairs for people on the fringes of survival—the poor, the lonely, the elderly, the forgotten. Teenagers transform cold, dark, decaying houses into warm, comfortable homes. But a workcamp experience changes more than just a house. It changes teenagers' lives.

- ♦ As teenagers improve the lives of others, they discover the power they have to change the world. By discovering what they can do, your kids' confidence in themselves will grow.
- ♦ Teenagers see firsthand what it means to be a victim of prejudice, poverty, or neglect. They explore different cultures. And they refine their own power to love others.
- ♦ As teenagers experience the power of being Christ's love in action, they have the opportunity to grow closer to Jesus.

A workcamp can help break the cycle of poverty, changing the lives of people trapped by it. Here's how:

- ♦ By easing the burdens of day-to-day survival, teenagers give people the chance to tackle other problems. For example, when kids build a wheelchair ramp for an elderly widow, she can then leave her house for a hot meal. Or when teenagers insulate a freezing shack, a young mother can then devote her attention to job training without worrying about her children's health.

- By improving living conditions, teenage workcampers help disadvantaged people build new self-esteem. Some poor children are so ashamed of their homes that they won't meet the school bus because they don't want others to see where they live. Substandard living conditions can make people feel too worthless to pursue an education or a job. A workcamp team gives people a new pride in where they live.
- By modeling a positive lifestyle, teenagers show people what they can achieve. Many families that have been caught in the cycle of poverty for generations may simply not know there are different ways to live. By serving as positive role models, teenagers can help others develop the desire to change their own lives.

In 1977, Group Workcamps innovated large-scale, organized workcamps. Since then, over 150 Group workcamps have been held across the United States and overseas, helping over 45,000 young people and their adult leaders grow closer to God.

To find out more about how to give your youth group the opportunity to participate in a summer workcamp, contact

Group Workcamps
Box 599
Loveland, CO 80539
(800) 774-3838

 **102**

YOUTH
-TO-
YOUTH

Drug-free zones and drug-free parties have emerged in an age in which alcohol and other drugs have become the norm at too many social gatherings. During the adolescent period of active experimentation, a significant number of young people choose to live drug-free. They still desire social gatherings and times of interaction; it's just that they want to be aware of what's going on during those times rather than being "bombed out."

An official organization called "Youth-to-Youth" (Y-2-Y) operates nationwide in the United States. The Seventh-day Adventist Church has worked with this agency and taken it worldwide.

It's usually a Youth-to-Youth convention that gets people excited and involved in Y-2-Y. At such a gathering, there are lots of young people, planned and structured times of interaction, "family groups" (a structure for small groups that provides support, sharing, interaction, and bonding), seminars about drugs and drug-free living, recreation, and more.

Local chapters at schools or churches can be formed to promote and provide a drug-free lifestyle. These chapters function as clubs that meet weekly as a "family group" and also plan drug-free social gatherings at least once a month. There's also the potential for joint activities with other Y-2-Y clubs and the annual conventions.

To find out more about Youth-to-Youth, contact

Institute of Alcohol and Drug Dependency
Andrews University
Berrien Springs, MI 49104

WE ARE HIS HANDS

Capo on 1st fret

Words and Music by
JEFF WOOD

1. We are His hands   to touch the world a - round   us.
2. We are His eyes   to   see the need in oth - ers.

We are His feet   to   go where He may lead,
We are His voice   to   tell of His re - turn,   and

we   are   His   love   burn - ing in the dark - ness.

We   are   His   love   shin - ing in the   night.

INDEX

Each of the 102 hands-on service ideas is listed with suggested stages (1–4) and whether the idea is recommended for inside the church community, outside the church community, or either/both. Many ideas can be used in more than one setting, and slight modification may make them more versatile.

Service Idea	Stages	In or Out	
29. CPR class	2	In	Out
30. Day camp	3	In	Out
31. Disaster response team (DaRT)	2, 4		Out
32. Drama group	4	In	Out
33. Encourage a politician	2		Out
34. Environmental awareness	3	In	Out
35. Environmental preservation	3, 4	In	Out
36. Family, group photos	2		Out
37. Family worship by you	2, 4	In	
38. Feed the homeless	2, 4		Out
39. Food closet—staffing	2, 4		Out
40. Food closet—stocking	2, 4		Out
41. Food merchants to food banks	2, 4		Out
42. Free car wash	2	In	Out
43. Freshmen orientation	2	In	Out
44. Fun Run	2, 3		Out
45. Gift wrapping	2		Out
46. Graffiti cleanup	2, 4		Out
47. Greeters at church	2, 3, 4	In	
48. Habitat for Humanity	3		Out
49. Home available	2, 4	In	
50. Hotline volunteers	4		Out
51. House cleaning service	3	In	
52. House repair scavenger hunt	2	In	Out
53. Immigrant ministry	3, 4	In	Out
54. Landscaping	2		Out
55. Letter of affirmation	2, 4	In	Out
56. Letters or cards for birthdays	4	In	
57. Letters to the editor	2	In	Out
58. Literature distribution	2, 4		Out
59. Missionary pen pal	4	In	
60. Moving day assistance	2	In	Out
61. Neighborhood Bible Club	2, 4	In	Out
62. Notes of encouragement	2, 4	In	Out
63. Office flower blitz	2		Out
64. Organ drive	2		Out
65. Outreach with other area churches	3, 4		Out
66. Parent-teen seminar	2, 3	In	

Service Idea	Stages	In or Out	
67. Parking meter mayhem	2		Out
68. Peer counseling	3, 4	In	Out
69. Person of the year banquet	3	In	Out
70. Plan a party	3	In	Out
71. Powder-puff car repair course	3	In	Out
72. Public servant appreciation day	2		Out
73. Radio or TV talk show	2, 4	In	Out
74. Rainy day curbside service	2	In	
75. Rake and run (or snow shovel and run)	2, 3	In	Out
76. Recycling program	4	In	Out
77. Rest areas	2, 3		Out
78. Runs or drives for the needy	3		Out
79. Senior citizen errands	2, 4	In	Out
80. Short-term mission trips	3	In	Out
81. Short-term mission trip welcome home party	2	In	
82. Smoking cessation program	3	In	Out
83. Social injustice	2, 3, 4	In	Out
84. Sponsor a child	4	In	Out
85. Sponsoring contests	3	In	Out
86. Sports clinics	2, 3	In	Out
87. Sports equipment drive	3	In	Out
88. Summer camp sponsor-a-kid	3	In	
89. Tapes of worship service	4	In	
90. Toy collection and distribution	2, 3		Out
91. Transportation service	2, 4	In	
92. Twelve-step program	4	In	Out
93. Vacation Bible School	3	In	Out
94. Vacation with a purpose	3	In	
95. Video contest	3	In	
96. Visitation program for missing youth	2, 3, 4	In	
97. Welcome wagon	2, 4	In	Out
98. Yard sale	2		Out
99. Youth auction	2	In	
100. Youth group service exchange	3, 4		Out
101. Youth group workcamps	3		Out
102. Youth-to-Youth	3	In	Out

Evaluation of *Hands-On Service Ideas for Youth Groups*

Please help Group Publishing, Inc., continue providing innovative and usable resources for ministry by taking a moment to fill out and send us this evaluation. Thanks!

● ● ●

1. As a whole, this book has been (circle one)

Not much help   Very helpful

1   2   3   4   5   6   7   8   9   10

2. The things I liked best about this book were:

3. This book could be improved by:

4. One thing I'll do differently because of this book is:

5. Optional Information:

Name _____

Street Address _____

City_____ State_____Zip_____

Phone Number _____Date _____

Group's
ReaL LIFe
B I B L E
CURRICULUM

Your Teenagers Need **Real** Hope...
Real Help...**Real** Answers...
So Give Them **Real Life Bible Curriculum**™

New From Group!

At last—hard-hitting, biblical, *one-session* topical studies for both your senior high *and* junior high/middle school students! Now you can...
- •Respond fast when kids bring up hot topics...
- •Have solid, biblical answers on hand for kids' tough questions...
- •Help teenagers discover for themselves what the Bible says...and
- •Give your group a balanced Bible overview!

Real Life—One Point.
Each **Real Life** study zeros in on one powerful, life-changing point—in-depth. And teenagers *apply* what the Bible teaches. Every activity...discussion...decision... drives home your lesson's biblical point—and challenges teenagers to respond.

Real Life—One Price.
Every lesson is the same low price. Add a few items from your home or classroom, and you have *everything* you need for *any* size class. No extra student books are required.

Real Life—One Promise.
Your teenagers will open up...talk...grow...and change...or your money back!

Topics include...

Junior High/Middle School:
The Case of the Empty Tomb   1-55945-527-6
Feeling Guilty: The Private Burden Kids Can't Shake
   1-55945-422-9
Helping Kids Be Better Friends   1-55945-534-9
I Would Die for You: Why Kids Stay in Gangs
   1-55945-417-2
Listen Up: Learning to Hear God's Answers to Prayer
   1-55945-415-6
The Making of the Bible   1-55945-419-9
Never Alone: God's Ultimate Answer to Loneliness
   1-55945-536-5
Personal Power   1-55945-525-X
Stairways to Heaven?: The Many Ways Kids Try to
   Reach God   1-55945-544-6
Too-Cool Kids: Survival Tactics of a Hurting
   Generation   1-55945-412-1
Why Do Bad Things Happen to Me?   1-55945-531-4

Senior High:
Buddha & Mohammed—Why Not?: The Awesome
   Impact of Jesus' Life on Earth   1-55945-526-8
The Diary of Teenage Runaways   1-55945-530-6
Dying to Live: The Messages of Kids Who Kill
   Themselves   1-55945-411-3
Jesus: Myth vs. Reality   1-55945-423-7
Jesus the Rebel   1-55945-414-8
Media Seduction: The Hi-Tech Battle for the Soul of a
   Generation   1-55945-413-X
No Pain, No Gain: How Painful Times Can Deepen
   Faith in God   1-55945-418-0
Sex Worth Waiting For: Learning to Treasure God's
   Powerful Gift   1-55945-528-4
Taking a Stand: Motivating Young People to Stand
   Up for Christ   1-55945-416-4
Teenage Romance: Positive Ways to Deal With the
   Ups and Downs of Relationships   1-55945-529-2
Understanding Why Churches Differ   1-55945-541-1
When Friends Fight: Helping Kids Resolve Conflict
   1-55945-420-2
When God Seems Silent   1-55945-532-2

...and many more!

Order today from your local Christian bookstore, or write: Group Publishing, Box 485, Loveland, CO 80539.